Tales of
A Musher

One Man's Fulfillment of His Alaskan Dream

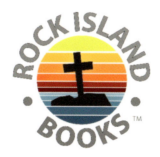

© 2016 William "Bill" Laughing-Bear

DEDICATION

I'd like to express my gratitude to CJ and Jo Ann Lovik who, sensing I was a living book, encouraged me to write my story. I am also indebted to the editor, my Mother, and to Josh Keely's finished fine-tuning of this overall project. A tremendous thanks goes to one of the greatest painters and illustrators of the 21st century, Adam Johnson.

A deep and heart felt thank you is in order for those who helped me launch my dream, encouraged me on and assisted in practical ways that proved to be divinely orchestrated as my new life took shape. Among those are my Dad, Gene, Gary, and for any I have overlooked, you know who you are.

A great big thank you goes to Charlie Boulding, the legendary musher known as "Easy Rider" and the first person I met after landing in Alaska. He headed me in the right direction for the rewarding and further pursuit of my life's dream. His encouragement spurred me on to live a simple life, one day at a time, and to keep 'first things first' which means following the *Great Mystery*.

And most importantly, I thank the *Great Mystery*, the indescribable Three-In-One.

Table of Contents

Chapter 1
At Long Last 9

Chapter 2
A New Beginning 19

Chapter 3
My New Companion 27

Chapter 4
But It Was Home! 39

Chapter 5
Alaskan Lessons I Learned The Hard Way 47

Chapter 6
No Cabin Fever For Me 53

Chapter 7
Four Legged Angel 59

Chapter 8
Heaves And BreakUps 63

Chapter 9
Mutual Foes And Picnics 69

Chapter 10
They Lied! 75

Chapter 11
Guess Who's Back? 79

Chapter 12
An Explosion Of Life 87

Chapter 13
Tiny Tormentors 93

Chapter 14
His Eyes Are On Me 97

Chapter 15
The Gentle Prompting 103

Chapter 16
The Dog House 111

Chapter 17
More Hard Earned Wisdom 119

Chapter 18
Beyond Belief 129

Chapter 19
Almost Too Good To Be True 137

Chapter 20
The Forest Fire 143

Chapter 21
Time For A Break! 149

Chapter 22
It Was (Another) God Thing 155

Chapter 23
And So Went The Winter 159

Chapter 24
The Team 165

Chapter 25
Just Every Day Alaska Living 171

Chapter 26
If I Had Only Stopped To Listen 177

Chapter 27
And Then… Finally!! 185

CHAPTER 1

At Long Last

"Wow, this Alaskan General Store is bigger than I imagined!" I couldn't believe I was finally in Fairbanks.

"I'm so hungry I could eat a moose, 'Alces alces,' all by myself," I muttered under my breath. All the cupboards in the little cabin I had rented were empty. As I gazed at all the people who were shopping in the general store, I noticed they were all wearing warm clothing. It suddenly dawned on me that stocking up on food was not the only challenge that lay ahead. It was already *the Moon of Leaves Turning Color*, or "September" as some of us Native Indians so poetically mused.

I thought I'd brought proper clothing to the *Land of the Midnight Sun*. As the temperature dropped in the following weeks I soon discovered that I was wrong! I simply was not prepared for the North Country.

I had spent hours researching my move to "the Last Frontier." There was one image that kept popping up, it was the image of the famous "Alaskan Bush Rats." To earn that title you must live and thrive deep in the wilds of what the Alaskans call the "Bush Country." To be called a "Bush Rat" was not an insult, it was a high compliment. It meant you were tougher than iron nails and had met the challenge of living in one of the most remote and unforgiving places in the entire world. The Bush Rat was the cream of the Alaskan crop, and meeting one was every Alaskan adventurers dream.

"Looks like you're lost. Can I help you find something?" I turned around and to my surprise I was face to face with what looked to me like the composite of every picture I had seen of the elusive Alaskan Bush Rat. He extended his hand and said, "Charlie Bouldings the name, what's yours? You look really lost. You just got here, didn't you?"

I shook his hand and introduced myself. I told him I came in just before midnight. I explained that I didn't really have a lot of money for a grub stake and had heard that this was the best place to stock up on bulk staples like beans, rice, flour, coffee, and the like. "It has been a life long dream for me to live in Alaska and I am determined to make a go of it." Charlie looked me in the eyes and gave me a wry, broad smile that told me that he understood my dream.

For the next hour plus Charlie asked me questions, listened to my story, and extended his friendship. He showed me where the food staples were and offered some much needed advise to help me stretch my skimpy resources.

Finally it was time to say goodbye to my new friend. We exchanged a firm handshake and Charlie provided a smile that was meant to give me encouragement, and it did.

Before Charlie left, he raised his right hand to get my

attention and said, "Bill, some men come up here and never become Sourdoughs, they will always be a Cheechako. And there are some who, from the moment they set foot in Alaska, are Sourdoughs." I nodded with a tight smile. Then Charlie continued, "I can tell you're a Sourdough even though you just got here, you've got the right attitude." My tight smile broadened as I immediately understood I had just been paid an enormous compliment. A Cheechako is an Indian term that means "tenderfoot." A Sourdough, on the other hand, was the slang term used in the Yukon Territory to describe someone who was a pioneer, a prospector, an adventurer. I was determined to be an Alaskan adventurer and Charlie had just made it official.

With that Charlie paused and then with a twinkle in his eye told me about some friends of his with whom I could meet and have coffee weekly. "These are good guys with their heads on straight and with the right attitude to make it here in Alaska. Nothing like solid friendships to help prevent cabin fever in the middle of the upcoming long winter."

I took mental notes of everything Charlie said and just when I thought he was out the door he turned around, took a couple of steps in my direction and said, "Remember Bill, if you want to make it up here…" he then paused as if to start parting words all over again. After taking a deep breath, he slowly began with a softer tone, "I'll leave you with this last little bit of advice." Charlie stroked his beard and in a somber tone that was meant to get my attention said, "Live a primitive, simple lifestyle without all the stuff, don't drink booze, take up mushing so you can trap, hunt, fish, haul your freight, and see the Bush. And most of all, keep first things first." I was later to find out that "keeping first things first" meant staying plugged in daily to the *Great Mystery*.

Over the next fifteen months I'd have many conservations with Charlie Boulding who had taken an interest in my success in this Great Land, Alaska, the land of my dreams. It was on my third visit with Charlie Boulding that I discovered that the "Bush Rat" I had met and struck up a friendship with was an Alaskan Legend.

The conversation on my third visit started and ended with the topic of mushing. Mushing is the exquisite combination of dogs bred to run long distances in the snow and ice with a sled that has developed over centuries to navigate through pathways of frozen tundra. Add a highly trained "musher" who has an intimate relationship with the terrain, a trusted relationship with the dogs and a durable sled and you have "mushing." Leave out any one of these three ingredients and you have a disaster just waiting to happen. Mushing is no less perilous than a 19th century ship captain taking a voyage into unchartered waters, both require a consumate skill, experience and confidence. Charlie Boulding was a legendary musher known far and wide by the sub-culture of all those who experienced the Alaska's wild first hand.

As I listened to Charlie discuss the wonders and challenges of mushing, I reached down and rubbed my right leg. Charlie picked up on the clue and stopped talking as he looked down to watch me adjust the brace that was hidden under my trousers. "You have a bad leg?" he asked in a concerned tone. I was embarrassed that I had interrupted Charlies description of the in and outs of mushing, looked up and answered. "Actually Charlie, I have two bad legs." I then told Charlie my own story. "I was run over by a vehicle while working as a Land Surveyor before coming to Alaska." After explaining a

few details, I then pulled my trouser leg up so Charlie could see the brace. "I have two of these contraptions attached to me," I complained. What happened next had me shaking my head with wonder. My Heavenly Father had done it again.

Instead of sympathy, Charlie looked at my brace and then began to chuckle. The chuckle soon became a laugh as Charlie reached over and patted me on the shoulder. This was followed by about 10 seconds of silence that seemed to roll on for an eternity. Finally the silence was broken. "Do you know what they call me," Charlie asked with a twinkle in his eye? "No sir," I answered. "They call me Easy Rider." What this meant, and what it had to do with my bad legs I did not know, but I was about to find out.

"Bill, I have the worst knees in the territory," Charlie stated as he patted his knees. "Now there are a few things in this life that just do not go together," he added. "You don't catch salmon with a frying pan, you don't dance with a Grizzly Bear, and you don't do much mushing with bad knees."

Charlie then went on to explain that he had been given the title of "Easy Rider" because he was the first one to figure out a way to incorporate a seat in his sled. This allowed him to go a long distance, and it allowed me to think about the possibility of mushing in spite of my bad legs. Charlie then leaned over as if to whisper in my ear, "don't let a gimp leg stop you, son. If I can do it, so can you." We both smiled.

Charlie exemplified the lifestyle of which I had only dreamed. He lived deep in the bush, ran a trapline, hunted, and caught hundreds of salmon with a fish wheel so he could feed his wife and dogs every year. He lived simply, yet maintained a healthy lifestyle full of adventure.

I am convinced beyond all doubt that Charlie Boulding was brought into my life by the "*Great Mystery.*" Who is the "*Great Mystery*" you might ask? If you haven't figured it out, you soon will.

I had rented a small log cabin and had begun slowly putting the pieces together in order to live the life of an Alaskan adventurer. This set the course for a life that has exceeded my wildest dreams.

As a lifelong outdoorsmen, I'd found my idealized dream

and have never looked back. On this adventure, which is still unfolding before me, I would have close encounters with Grizzly bears, wolves, "Canis lupus," and moose. There would be countless salmon to catch, the mushing of dogs underneath Northern Lights, and encounters that brought friendships with some of the best people on the planet. But most of all, I would find a walk so close to the *Great Mystery*, "God the Father," that He would become my best friend as I learned to see His fingerprints and hear His whisper.

So as I sit at my manual typewriter, stories dart about my mind much like the oil lamps flicking on my cabin's walls as if they were dancing. The first story I would like to share has nothing to do with bears, caribou, "Rangifer tarandus," rangifer tarandus, or blizzards. It has to do with something even bigger. The adventure that has captured my imagination and has never dimmed happened when I was given the rare privilege of actually seeing the fingerprints of the *Great Mystery* as I prepared to make my way north to Alaska. It happened while deep in the Interior of Canada traveling the Alcan Highway.

CHAPTER 2

A New Beginning

If anyone needed a fresh start it was me. My dream had always been to live in Alaska. My world as I knew it had disintegrated. I had little money and an old Bronco that was the perfect size to carry some but not all the tools and supplies I still owned. I took the matter in prayer to the *Great Mystery*, and less than a week later my friend and father figure, Gene Dale, showed up with a message. "Bill," he said "you should follow your dream and move to Alaska." "But Gene,"

A New Beginning

I protested, "that takes money that I simply do not have." Gene smiled as he placed an envelope in my hand. "This is enough cash to get you there, if you're careful, and a small grubstake to help you get by for a little while." Now a grubstake is not a gift, it is money or supplies advanced to a prospector or trapper in return for a share of his findings. Gene then reassured me with these words, "there's no interest due, just pay me back if you can some day."

I was in shock. This had the fingerprint of the *Great Mystery* all over it. I had not asked for this loan but Gene had felt in his heart that this was what he needed to do.

Just a few days later, I was contacted and told of a cabin I could rent in Fairbanks. Yes, they would hold it for me. One more fingerprint and then there was a third. My friend, Gary Griffiths, called, "Hey Bill, I've got this small trailer you can have. You might be able to take a few more things with you."

A third fingerprint. I had not sought a trailer, this was given to me as a gift. So without even asking, I had been provided a way to transport my carpenter's toolbox, mechanic's tool box, and a few other things that would come in very handy.

A New Beginning

As the big day of my adventure of a lifetime approached, I loaded everything up. "Something is missing," I thought. I did not know why but I decided I just had to carry my bucket of nuts, bolts, and washers, nails and screws. As I was loading it into my new trailer, a couple of my friends who had shown up to help told me, "you don't need that." I paused for a moment but finally yielded to the nudge I was getting in my spirit to take that bucket of nuts and bolts along. "You never know when the odd screw or bolt might come in handy in my Alaskan cabin," I reported back to my friends. They just shrugged and smiled.

After a dinner with friends and my Mum, I crawled into my sleeping bag, said a prayer of thanks and went to sleep.

The next morning, after a hardy breakfast, I threw my sleeping bag into the truck, and headed for the Canadian Border.

 Upon arrival at the Canadian entry station, I asked the Border Guard if after they inspected my truck and trailer, I could park and tarp off the trailer? The Canadian Border Guard asked, "What is your destination?" "Fulfilling a dream and moving to Fairbanks, Alaska," I reported with a smile.

He smiled back and cautiously replied, "Well, I can't let you across unless you take this pin." I was caught off guard. "Excuse me," I replied. The Border Guard waved me forward and as I approached him he unpinned the Canadian flag pendant from his uniform and pinned it on my shirt. "Where is your camera?" he asked. I rustled through my glove compartment and produced my camera. The next thing I knew the Guard had taken my camera and clicked off a couple of pictures before he handed it back to me. Then the Guard said, "keep the pin as a memory, have a wonderful trip." I had heard horror stories of what could happen at the border crossings and realized that "Someone" had given me favor. Someone seemed to be reminding me that He was right by my side. As I tarped off the trailer and made my way into Canada, I could not help but turn my thoughts to the *Great Mystery*, and how He was constantly reminding me of His near presence. Just like that I was through the border with everything I owned in the world.

The trip was slow since my little rig was really underpowered. I became aware of just how underpowered every time I had to climb the passes. Since I had no money to stay in motels or to eat in roadside cafés, I just kept motoring along as

A New Beginning

I ate meals my Mum had prepared for me. I was road weary and needing a rest, but the temperature dropped when I stopped to rest so I just kept motoring onward.

Everything was going slow but smooth and then suddenly I found myself in distress. On the last full day of driving through Canada, disaster struck. I was to be shown the *Great Mysteries* fingerprints in a way that stunned me and brought me to my knees.

For miles I had had to slowly struggle through new road construction. It was so bad I had to lock in my four-wheel-drive because it was so muddy and rough. Then, in the cold and dark, I realized the trailer's box was sliding sideways off the frame. I pulled over with a sinking feeling that made me sick! I got out and, standing in several inches of mud, inspected the mess. Welds had given way even though I'd been crawling along at about five miles an hour. I was miles from help, there was no help! I realized there were holes which, if I could get them aligned, would allow me to bolt the box back to the frame. I could use a pry bar. I had to shove the box, but where could I get the nuts, bolts, and washers needed to adhere this all together? Then very clearly, I heard a whisper, "You have that bucket I had you throw into the trailer along with your tools. You see, I knew you would need them."

Yes, it took some time to un-tarp so I could dig out all I needed. And it was cold and I was laying in mud that even packed into my hair, but I was able to patch things together and slowly get back on the road once again.

As I motored along that night, I had an overwhelming understanding that the Creator was watching over me. I remembered a passage written in the "Biggest Book" in Psalms 27:5:

"For He will hide me in his shelter in the day of trouble; he will conceal me under the cover of his tent; he will lift me high upon the rock."

 He had known I was going to be in need of a bucket that had what I needed in the middle of nowhere with no one around to help me. My Heavenly Father made sure I had the resources I needed. He made sure I was covered.

That bucket was smeared with my muddy fingerprints before the job of securing the box to the trailer was finished.

A New Beginning

When it was all done, I realized that the bucket also had His fingerprints all over it. I never thought God could use a rusty bucket of nuts and bolts to bring me to my knees. But He did! I still own that bucket to this day and have kept it as a reminder of how much my Heavenly Father cares for me.

A New Beginning

CHAPTER 3

My New Companion

I soon discovered how friendly and helpful Alaskans can be. But it didn't take me long to figure out that living in the backwoods of Alaska required more than human friendship. I needed a dog, "Canis lupus familiaris," and I needed one right away.

It was going to be a big decision, a lifetime commitment. I immediately took it to my Heavenly Father, the *Great Mystery*. Without finances this was going to be a real challenge. Well… a challenge for me, but not for my Heavenly Father.

It was true that the companionship of a good dog is a wonderful thing. In Alaska it is also a very necessary thing. Every time you step outside in the Alaskan back woods you're putting yourself in harms way. A good dog that has developed an inseparable bond with its Alpha Pack Leader will not only lay it's life down to protect its master, it will also warn of impending dangers that humans simply are not equipped to recognize.

As a First Nation's man, I had been taught to always pay attention to ravens, "Corvus corax," Red squirrels, "Tamiasciurus hudsonicus," and dogs because they are very accurate alarms systems. If these critters are putting up a fuss, there is probably something wrong. There was no doubt about it, I really needed a good dog.

As I made this a matter of prayer, I remembered my last of many encounters with a "Ursus americanus," otherwise known as an American Black Bear.

I was on an outdoor adventure in the lower 48 plus 1. As a point of interest, you might like to know that Hawaii is lower than Alaska making the grand total of 49 states lower than Alaska. Anyway, I was camping in the woods with one of my friends and after a long exhausting day of hiking we had retired to our tent. We were trying to get some sleep when we were attacked by an American Black Bear. To be more accurate, our tent was attacked and torn to shreds. We survived, my tent didn't.

I was now living in the Land of the Midnight Sun. Alaska boasts one living beast that is much more troublesome than the American Black Bear that roams the lower 49. His name is "Ursus arctos horribilis." Just the name gives you a giant clue that this is no ordinary beast.

A full-grown Grizzly Bear can stand over seven feet tall at the shoulders and weigh eight hundred and fifty pounds. I have seen claws that were over four inches in length. Grizzlies have been clocked running at thirty-five miles per hour. How fast can you run? Probably faster than me, but not fast enough to escape an advancing Grizzly that has you in its sites. Thirty-five miles an hour might not seem fast if you're driving in a car down the freeway but in the woods of Alaska, thirty-five miles an hour is "greased lightening" with giant claws and teeth. If I was going to live in the Alaskan Bush, I was definitely going to need a very good dog.

My New Companion

Since I had little money, I prayed and pondered the dog issue for several days. Finding a good dog at the animal shelter was highly unlikely and seemed a waste of time. Yet I kept feeling a nudge to investigate. I had learned to listen to these quiet whispers and gentle nudges that the *Great Mystery* so often used to direct my path. I wasn't very hopeful but I was off to the shelter.

I arrived at the animal shelter early the following afternoon. I was looking for a good Alaskan dog that could handle the harsh Alaskan winter. I carefully previewed all the available dogs and found none of them suitable for the rugged wilderness living that was on my near horizon.

The thought that I was wasting my time did cross my mind, but then I noticed something a little distance from the shelter. I saw a very large, beautiful Akita. My hopes were slighty revived until, upon investigation, I was told this dog was unavailable for adoption. She was in a penned up area where a close up view of her was prohibited. I immediately returned to the shelter and began making inquiries regarding the dog. I was told the reason she was in the separate pen was because she had just been delivered. The animal shelter had a policy that pets put in the shelter were kept apart from the rest of the dogs so the former owner had an opportunity to come back and retrieve the dog if they had a change of heart.

I was not the only one interested in this prized animal. Many other families who showed up had also made inquiries about her. All were told the same thing I had been told and no one had been allowed to approach her.

For the biggest part of the day this magnificent animal lay on top of the doghouse next to where she was staked. As I gazed at her, I realized she reminded me of an African lion. She was stately in appearance, very calm, and nothing seemed to escape her stare.

I decided I was not going anywhere until I had exhausted every chance of obtaining this animal who had captured my attention and was already worming its way into my heart. This provided me lots of time to pray and observe. I was not the only one doing the observing. The Akita locked eyes with me and would not let me out of her gaze. All afternoon long she watched me. When I wandered off a bit she went into alert mode and watched me leave. When I would return she fixed her gaze on me. I observed that she did not do this with the others who mingled around the compound; she'd glance at them and then lock eyes with me once more. I noticed one more thing that impressed me greatly. She never made a sound, not a whimper, not a bark, not a sigh. She was always composed and despite being in a strange place she kept her composure and her dignity. The more I saw of her, the more I liked what I saw.

Was time on my side? I didn't know. Was I wasting my time by circling the animal shelter hoping for some sign that this was all going to work out? I wondered.

Later that afternoon when there was a change of staff I entered the animal shelter again, just hoping for a chance to look her over. I received the same response, "she is not available." I was getting discouraged. But, I remained vigilant. Nothing comes to the impatient except disappointment. I had learned that lesson in life and was determined to keep my hopes fresh as long as any sliver of hope remained.

I looked at my pocket watch. The animal shelter was going to close in less than thirty minutes. Had I wasted an entire day hoping the impossible would happen?

I had come to the conclusion that the answer to that question was, yes. I was about to leave when the slight nudge that directed me to the shelter in the first place turned into a nudge and a whisper. "Bill, go and ask about this dog one more time." "You're just day dreaming," I said to myself. "Don't be stupid, you've asked twice before." Despite my protests, I could not shake the urge to listen to the small voice that kept urging me to give it one more try. Finally, and rather sheepishly, I went to ask about the Akita one more time.

As I entered the shelter and approached the counter, I noticed a new face I had not seen before.

Trying to smile and with a small lump in my throat, fully expecting to be rebuffed for my persistance, I leaned over the counter. "Ma'am, I've been here since early afternoon watching that Akita. Now I realize she can't be adopted because she is on hold, but when could I come back and adopt her?"

What happened next reminded me again that I was not in this adventure alone. The pathway was being cleared of ob-

stacles in a realm I could not see with my physical eyes, but no one can convince me it is not just as, or more real than the hardwood counter top I had rested my elbows on.

The woman looked at me and said, "Do you mean to tell me that Akita is still in the holding pen." I said, "Yes, Ma'am. She has been there all afternoon." She turned to the staff and yelled, "Why is that Akita still in the holding pen? She was to be available first thing this morning. Now get her out so this man can adopt her, now!" There was no doubt that I was face to face with the person who ran the shelter.

Two other families immediately spoke up saying they wanted her as well. The response from the boss, who had the bearing of a Marine Drill Sergeant, was polite but firm. "Sorry folks, but she is already spoken for."

She then gave me a knowing look like she had just done me a big favor. If she only knew how true that was. She then began the process that ended with the adoption of the dog I had prayed for.

Adoption is one of the specialities of Heaven, and I had

just been given a picture of how much I was loved by my Heavenly Father, the *Great Mystery*. I knew I had been adopted by the Father because of the Cross work done on Calvary by His Son. Now I was getting a little taste of what adoption was all about.

So just before closing, I signed all the paperwork. I was then presented with a hundred and thirty pound, fit and healthy Akita that had not an ounce of fat on her. I was told that her previous family was in the military and had been given orders to deploy to Germany. I decided to call her Ally. This proved to be the perfect name to describe the perfect dog.

Ally was just getting ready to turn two years old. She had been well loved and very well trained by a master who was a military police officer. His job was to train dogs for police and security service, and Ally was proof of his talent. What a gift I had been given.

I have learned that when God gives you something special, He is honored when you treat it with love and respect. There is actually a way to do that.

The first way is to never forget to thank your Heavenly Father for the gifts He has given you. How easily we take all His benefits for granted and become like the stiff necked people of God in the wilderness having just been set free from the bondage of Egypt. How easy it is to forget all the benefits our Heavenly Father, the *Great Mystery*, has heaped like treasure into our lives.

I have learned that while thanking God out loud, screaming it at the top of our lungs so everyone can hear about it is one way of showing gratitude, but there is another way that is even more important. That way is to cherish and care for what He has given you.

I was determined to take good care of Ally. I figured if the *Great Mystery* went to such great lengths to let me know that it was He alone Who arranged my adoption of Ally, the least I could do was honor Him by the constant and daily act of appreciation displayed by my care of her.

Ally gave me the desire to become the man she thought I was, for it says in Proverbs 12:10, "Whoever is righteous has regard for the life of his beast, but the mercy of the wicked is cruel."

My New Companion

For you see, a man who seeks the *Great Mystery* has a kind heart and is kind toward his animals! I had been given the blessing of Ally who I would soon learn was even better than I could imagine. I had been taught that the good is the enemy of the best!

There were other good dogs out there but the Great Father had wanted me to have the best dog, a dog that would watch and protect me. A dog that would end up saving my life, and not just once. In the final analysis it was the *Great Mystery*, my Heavenly Father, Who was looking after me and preserving me from injury and death. Ally was His messenger of mercy. This is something I'll never forget.

Psalms 68:19

Blessed be the Lord, who daily loadeth us with benefits, even the God of our salvation. Selah.

CHAPTER 4

But It Was Home!

I loved my little cabin, and by little, I mean little. With Ally living inside, it was cozy. When a friend would come to visit it was snug. If he brought a friend with him it was crowded. More than three visitors and you felt like a Grizzly Bear in a phone booth.

I had always wanted to live in a real log cabin. As I looked out the small window I could see the valley was displaying the vibrant colors the Creator had brushed on the landscape to whisper to the world that it was the end of a season. I waited with anticipation for the first snow that announced fall was over and winter was about to begin.

The furnishings were a little sparse, but I was home. I had a military cot that did double duty as my bed and couch, my sleeping bag, and a three-legged stool. I had a small kerosene camp stove, an oil lamp, and some camping cookware. With a little effort I made a table, put up some shelves, and scrounged up a couple more chairs.

The cozy log cabin was next to a river. While others watched television for entertainment I watched the beavers, "Castor canadensis," from my porch that was only about fifteen feet from the waters edge. Trout and grayling jumped up to see what was going on in my world and they just as quickly slipped back into water. Every once in a while a river otter, "Lutra lutra," would pass by. But the biggest treat I saw that first winter on the river was a Marten, "Martes americana." The resourceful marten had located an old beaver who had died. This provided nourishment to the marten, and hours of entertainment for me. When only scraps were left my favorite bird, the raven, joined the feast.

This cabin was built up on pilings and stood about three feet off the ground. It was what the Alaskans called a dry cabin which meant it had no running water. Many locations in Alaska do not have running water because it's just too expensive to install. The permafrost (ground that is permanently frozen) is an expensive obstacle to overcome, and overcoming it can cost as much as building the rest of the cabin.

All my water came from the nearby town of Fox. It was named well since if you blinked you missed it, just like spotting the illusive fox. Everything is known for something and Red Fox, "Vulpes vulpes." is known for a pipe that comes up out of the ground, gushing pure water all year round. The water springs from an artesian well (one in which the water flows to the surface naturally). This water was not only the best water I had ever tasted, but it was free to anyone in need.

As the ice builds up, all winter the State of Alaska comes in with a machine that "steams" things to help remove the ice from high traffic areas. Even with this you had to wear cleats or spikes on your boots to prevent yourself from slipping and falling.

On many of my weekly trips to "water up," I would end up helping the aged and women who were alone getting their water jugs filled and placed in their trucks. They could not do it on their own because it was too slippery on the ice, and they did not have cleats on their boots. I was not the only good Samaritan in the Interior of Alaska. Most Alaskans live by the golden rule and take great care to look after their neighbors. It reminded me often of what is written in the Biggest Book in Luke 10:25-35.

One of the distinquishing features of a "Sourdough" is his willingness to help a stranger or a neighbor even though it will cost him, expecting nothing in return. This is what real Alaskans do!

I was shortly to get a lesson that you could only learn in Alaska. It began at the time of *the Snow Moon,* or "November." I was standing in the cabin when all of sudden it jolted straight up and then began to sway like a reed in the wind. It shook so bad I could not stand up and fell to the floor. It seemed like an eternity before I was finally able to get off the floor to scramble outside to see what was going on. Attached to my cabin there was a massive porch and

But It Was Home!

a stones throw away from that was the Outhouse. What I saw were trees whipping back and forth like flags in a hurricane. I seriously thought the cabin was going to come off its pilings.

My Bronco was bouncing off the ground, appearing to be at times two feet in the air as it skipped all over the yard like an over caffeinated energizer bunny. I actually had to run away from it as it hopped toward me.

I learned this was caused by the largest inland earthquake to hit Alaska in one hundred and fifty years. It was a whopping 7.9 on the Richter scale.

It caused the cabin to lean hard and settle about ten inches lower in the southwest corner. My cabin now had a tilt that only had one benefit as far as I could see, every morning I knew exactly where to find Ally's ball because it would roll into the corner.

The following spring the damage was repaired and the cabin was re-leveled. This made cooking and doing dishes a lot easier. Living in a small cabin in Alaska is challenging enough, but living in a lopsided cabin is downright annoying. Fortunately, during the earthquake, the stove inside my cabin stayed in place and that was a real blessing. My fuel line and tank that was bolted down stayed in place and did not spill the stove oil that I relied on for all my cooking and heating. Later I heard tales of more than one Alaskan chasing their lit stoves all over their cabins trying to put the roaring fires out. All things considered, I had lived through it with little damage or inconvenience. Not everyone was so blessed.

The big quake had caused landslides, damaged railroad tracks and roads. The next day I saw one semi-truck that was in bad shape after being thrown off the road, leaning partially on its side where the pavement had given way beneath it.

My friend, Shannon Rice, was a trucker who would bring in loads of freight from the lower forty-nine. Just after the earthquake, when he arrived at a weigh station, he angrily chewed out the staff declaring, "these road conditions are unacceptable." He told them there were cracks so wide and deep you could roll a truck onto its side. Since big rigs are not overly smooth to ride in, he had not realized that just before he got there, the land had been rocked. He said he was just guessing he'd hit a rough stretch of road that was moving him all over the place although he could not really see what had caused such a bumpy ride. He was the first one to report these conditions and the Alcan was closed shortly after for repairs.

I have often pondered that day that the earth seemed to be coming apart. Although there have been many earthquakes experienced since then, this was my first one and I will never forget it.

Very little has ever unnerved me, but I do not mind saying that the day the "big one" hit Alaska, I was terrified. I called out, no, I yelled out to the *Great Mystery* to protect me.

Can you imagine the sheer terror that will be much more amplified on the day the Seventh bowl is poured out upon the earth by the seventh angel as it is written about in the Biggest Book in Revelation 16:17-20?

Those who know the *Great Mystery* through His Son, Jesus the Christ, will be gone from this earth and will not have to live through those days recorded in Revelation 16 when even the bravest hearts will melt in terror because they have no relationship with the Savior.

CHAPTER 5

Alaskan Lessons I Learned The Hard Way

As the last of the leaves blanketed the already frozen ground, the hoarfrost began to take over everything.

Hoarfrost can grow to a depth of several inches and is beyond beautiful, especially as sunshine makes it sparkle like untold millions of frozen diamonds.

The oil drip stove required no electricity to operate the thermostat. You just turned it on to where you found it the most comfortable and the heating oil just trickled into the burning pot. I soon found living in a log cabin built up off the ground had an oddity I'd never experienced.

I like to keep the temperature about seventy degrees, which kept it very comfortable. My inside attire was usually Carhartt jeans and a tee shirt. The floors were cold and frost hugged the inside walls all winter long to the height of about a foot off the floor. I had to wear either my winter boots on the floor or extremely heavy wool socks and sheep skin slippers. Otherwise, my feet would hurt from the cold.

I discovered that in this extremely dry cold, I could not make a snowball. The snow would just sift through my hands like sugar. The upside was that it was easy to brush off when I fell in it or some tumbled out of a tree onto my parka. I just brushed it off, not having to worry about getting wet.

I had heard my "coffee buddies" discuss some interesting things you could do in sub zero weather. For example, you could take a boiling cup of coffee and throw it into the air and it would come down as ice crystals. A rather expensive experiment, but I just had to do it a couple of times for the record. A poor mans ice thrill was to spit and listen to it pop as it froze before it hit the ground. I didn't do a lot of spitting, and coffee was a luxury I did not want to squander but I just had to know if the "coffee clutch" was telling me the truth or just having fun with a newbie. As it turned out, they were telling the truth.

I learned the hard way to always wear at least a liner glove whenever touching a metal object. I had been working outside for a long period of time and needed my pocketknife. I could not open the folding blade with my mittens on so I took them off, much to my regret. As I was opening the blade, a searing, burning sensation made me drop my knife. Going inside, I watched my fingers as they blistered from burning them on the subzero knife blade. I made a note to myself, "never touch anything metal again without at least wearing a liner glove." I soon learned that it was wise, when outside, to wear a liner glove inside my mittens at all times.

I remember one night while at an outside hot spring beneath the Northern Lights, I would go under the water and as

I would come up from the heated paradise of tranquility, I'd grab my hair and pull it up like horns where it would freeze and stay pointing toward the starry host.

As I left the pool, heading for the building, a friend who was goofing off slapped me on the chest - all in fun. The next morning when I awoke and looked into my mirror, I saw a clear handprint where the chest hair had just simply broken off.

The Bronco did not always start even though I had installed an oil pan heater, a block heater, and an electric battery blanket. There were many days that I just wasn't going anywhere. And when I did get it to fire up, after a long warmup, I'd have a bouncy ride because all four tires were frozen out-of-round from sitting. It would usually take two to three miles of an odd bump-bounce for them to warm enough to smooth out the ride. So when I did have it on the road, I made the best of it since I wasn't sure when this would happen again. I'd fill water jugs, do needed shopping, hit the laundry mat for a shower and wash my clothes. And of course, I'd get together with other like-minded friends and share the excitement I'd found living the life that my friend, Charlie Boulding, had encouraged me to live. Yep, I was doing most of it but I was missing one critical link. I needed a mushing dog team!

Alaskan Lessons I Learned The Hard Way

CHAPTER 6

No Cabin Fever For Me

That first year there was a lack of snow in Willow, Alaska, where the restart of the Iditarod dog sled race begins after its ceremonial start in Anchorage. It was decided the race would have to have its restart in Fairbanks. I made plans to be standing on the frozen river in *the Moon of Snowblind*, "March," as the mushers came by. I was excited! I had not yet been close to a dog team so I waited with anticipation for the Easy Rider to come tearing down the trail that was on the river. I remember thinking "these dogs look like a team, like they belong together, not like so many people who are all about being number one, on top, all by themselves."

When I saw Charlie coming down the trail, I cheered so loud I wondered if the ice I was standing on would crack. Charlie waved and slipped by with what I felt sure was the finest dog team I had seen that day. I was hooked from that day forward. I knew that one day, I'd have my own dog team and wear a yellow anorak, just like this man who so inspired me.

Of all the things I have had the privilege to witness that the *Great Mystery* has created, the Aurora's are at the very top of the list, even better than snow! When the two merge, I feel like I'm in Heaven, especially when viewed from the runners of a dogsled.

Often while mushing, I have wondered about those who live in places where snow doesn't fall. Can they truly visualize and take to heart one of my all-time favorite verses found in Isaiah 1:18? "Come now, let us reason together says the Lord; Though your sins are like scarlet, they shall be as white as snow; though they are red like crimson, they shall become like wool." Or even Psalm 51:7, "Purge me with hyssop, and I shall be clean; wash me, and I shall be whiter than snow." How do they wrap their minds around snow without having seen it?

Cabin fever can be a real problem for many, especially on long, dark winter days when there is a lack of Vitamin D from enough sunlight. People often fight depression, are discontent, put things off until tomorrow, and some even become aggressive. Most of us are outside and very active in winter which helps keep it at bay. Eating healthy food, getting proper rest, and keeping an active mind also helps.

By doing that, plus getting my vitamin D as I sit each morning when I have my quiet time in the light of an Aladdin Genie oil lamp, cabin fever has remained far from me. These lamps produce a purer quality light more closely resembling sunshine than the "sad" lights many buy to help fight this problem. I also believe that working to have a good attitude is a must so I try to be positive and dwell on good things like it says we are to do in the Biggest Book in Philippians 4:6-8.

That first winter it became my habit to put on heavy, winter clothing and boots and sit on the porch while being mesmerized by the Northern Lights as they filled the sky like a curtain of dancing angels. Often I would see green, white, red, yellowish, purplish, and even a bluish-colored light. When things are just right and you are remote, away from all sound, occasionally you can hear the lights. It sounds something like a crackling sound or static from an old radio that is not on frequency. I have yet to not have them calm me when I am stressed or have had a rough day. Many times I would go for a walk, sometimes tripping since I wasn't watching where I was going because I was looking up into the heavens. At times they were so bright they seemed to cast shadows around me and there was no need for my headlamp. Later in life, I almost lost a dog team as I was watching one of the best light shows ever. I hit a bump, fell off, and had to grasp the snubline (a rope attached to the front of the sled, which can be tied to a tree to hold the team) that drags behind my sled, pulling myself hand over hand back toward the sled runners as I bounced along the trail behind the team while screaming, "whoa!"

I enjoyed that first winter, taking in many events such as the ice carving championships and the Yukon Quest dog sled race that runs between Fairbanks, Alaska and White Horse,

Canada in *the Moon of Wind Scattering Leafs Over the Snow Crust,* "February." I learned that it was a thousand mile race and Easy Rider was the first to ever win twice.

No Cabin Fever For Me

CHAPTER 7

Four Legged Angel

People in this north land often grill moose, caribou, and salmon outside even if it is forty below zero. Evenings with friends became the norm and I talked to anyone I could about trapping because this provides a Bush Rat with clothing, food for his dogs and himself, and some possible income.

One day I invited Nikki over for coffee and lunch to talk hunting and trapping. She is one of the toughest and most qualified Alaskans I have ever met. At times she drove a big rig (a semi-trailer truck), was a carpenter, and had even built her own cabin.

As she approached my cabin, a moose suddenly burst through some heavy brush that was so covered in hoarfrost it had blocked our view. As this moose charged, Ally dove off the porch and bolted toward it. I do not remember grabbing my 12-guage, but one moment it wasn't in my hands and all of a sudden it was and I was looking down the barrel at this charging moose. I kept my shotgun with slugs over the cabin door because to bring it inside when the metal was cold would bring on condensation and invite rust.

Nikki tripped and fell about ten feet shy of the porch as Ally ran past her and locked up with the moose. As Ally weaved in and out, the moose lost focus of Nikki and she crawled under my cabin. With her out of the way, I fired a round next to the moose as a warning shot and jacked in the next round ready to send the 525-grain slug into its chest. I had paused before firing at first because unless there was no other choice, I did not want to fire a slug close to my friend as she ran.

Four Legged Angel

Between Ally and the resounding roar of the twelve gauge, the moose turned and bolted away faster than he'd come. I called Ally back and helped Nikki up onto the porch. Yep, you guessed it! That night Ally ate moose steak and as I recall, I believe Nikki supplied it. That day, Ally was for us a four legged angel.

CHAPTER 8

Heaves And BreakUps

Because the earthquake had been very unsettling to me, any jolt to the cabin immediately grabbed my attention. That first winter, another new facet of the far north, frost heaves, made my heart skip a beat more than once.

Much of Alaska has permafrost under it. Basically, the ground is frozen beneath a few inches of topsoil year-round. In the extreme north this can be to a depth of two thousand feet. In my area, at times the ground would just heave and crack, giving a little jolt. I could go out to where I had parked my rig and see the cracks running across the packed-down snow.

Sometimes roads would heave upwards so much you would go airborne when hitting them. In Canada, they only put out red flags to mark the worst ones. My trip up was very exciting the first time I accidentally found one as I was trying to understand what the flag was all about. As the Bronco hit one and the trailer flew up, it seemed like I would never land. I believe angels were guiding the truck because I was all over the road and almost lost control when I landed. Somehow it straightened out but my nerves were all over the place for some time. For the rest of the trip, when I'd spot a flag, I slowed down well below the posted speed limit sign. In Alaska, when they appear, the road department does their best to put up warning signs.

The days became longer as spring approached. Soon Breakup was upon the land as the snow melted, roads turned to mud, and the world overnight seemed to turn green. I started venturing further north where I saw bears with new cubs, and by May new moose calves began to appear. Although most cows have two calves, occasionally I'd see three and one time I saw one with four calves.

The cows had quite the attitude and if one is wise, they always carry the 12-guage when outside (which I learned the hard way). I had a cow chase me into the outhouse and she would not let me leave. I'd watch and when she would wander a little ways away, I'd try to slip out and make a dash for the cabin. But faster than lighting she would thunder back toward me, snorting and stomping her hooves. It took the bulk of the afternoon before I was able to reach the safety of the cabin. I was really starting to get a little cold because I had not dressed for such a long time away from the cabin.

As the summer crested, I panned for gold in the streams, explored the next ridge, and took my truck to places it should never have gone. Fishing was wonderful and my garden really took off growing. One afternoon I found the beavers in it. I think they ate more of it than I did because when Ally was away with me, they just helped themselves to this ready made salad bar.

I went camping a lot but had a hard time sleeping because of the continuous light. It seemed odd to sit around a campfire at midnight, fully able to see everything without a flashlight. And the lack of stars at night, well, it just seemed… wrong!

After living in the Interior a year, I took one of my road trips and headed south to what many call "Alaska's Play Land," the Kenai Peninsula. Although I was told it wasn't as cold there as the Interior, it was next to Cook Inlet where I would have chances for salmon and salt water fishing.

One big drawback was the bigger bears. They had loads of Brown Bears, "Ursus arctos," that can easily reach lengths longer than eight feet and be over four and a half feet at the shoulders. Some can weigh fifteen hundred pounds or more.

I was awestruck by what I saw and decided I'd move south and give it a try for a full year. I believe one needs to stay put at least a year so they can see what it is like through all four seasons. So, within *the Moon of Popping Trees*, or "December," I loaded everything including my sidekick, Ally, and headed south a little over five hundred miles.

My friend, Denali, one of my "coffee gang" told me, "I'm telling my friend, Bob, down there in Soldotna, you're moving south. He'll keep an eye out for you. Check in with him when you get there and he'll introduce you to some other great guys." So, I did just that.

    Within days I was settled into the small place I'd rented and started hunting Snowshoe Hare, "Lepus americanus," and Rock Ptarmigan, "Lagopus mutus," for my dinners. I liked living a few miles distance from the smaller town of Soldotna. But little did I realize that in this corner of Alaska, the excitement was just about to begin!

Heaves And BreakUps

CHAPTER 9

Mutual Foes And Picnics

Upon moving to the Kenai I ran into a new foe, the moose with a hatred for dogs. I had just settled into my new cabin when a moose started giving me grief. It spotted Ally right off the get-go and charged. We slammed the door to the inside of the cabin shut and it stomped its hooves at the door. When opening the door, after the moose had wandered off, it would come charging back. For the next several weeks, if it was within viewing range of the cabin and it spotted Ally and me, it would close in on us. It did not matter if we had just driven into the driveway, if we were outside for any reason and were spotted, it would come running.

None of the other moose we encountered did this, but apparently this moose had been harassed by dogs in the past and simply hated them. It became quite the challenge at times to let Ally out to do her business, or to get into the truck to make a road trip. I had to be on constant guard. With this moose being a continuous problem, Ally decided that moose were her foes and she hated them all. Although she would not chase after them, she would stand her ground and not back down. Eventually, she would take on more than one as she guarded her human.

I finally used rubber buckshot which stings but does not inflict lethal damage to drive this moose away. I learned that first winter on the Kenai that firing a warning shot would often help once or twice to send a moose or bear on its way, but it was a short-term answer. In short order they get used to the sound and not leave when one embarked on a noise campaign with a thunderstick (a hunting rifle or a shotgun. Natives first called them that because of their 'thundering' sound).

It took a little time but I settled into my new cabin, which was much smaller than the one I'd left in Fairbanks. In *the Big Wind Moon*, or "April," I started having trouble with a bull moose that would not leave us alone. One evening, all of a sudden, Ally, who was on a cable run outside the cabin, sounded off with a resounding, deep bark. I got up and looked out the window to see if that bull moose that kept coming after her was back.

There was no bull moose but one massive Brown Bear was headed straight for my dog. Well, this wasn't going to happen, regardless of how big it was! I grabbed the 12-gauge full of magnum slugs and out the door I bolted. The bear, by this time, was less than 10 feet from my girl who looked about the size of a poodle up against a Great Dane, and... Ally was not backing down! I really didn't want to have to kill this bear because I love having them around, and all I could think of was "please don't move, I need to go get my camera."

The bear started closing in on her but she just knew she was going to destroy that bear. She showed no fear whatsoever! I pulled the trigger on my thunderstick and placed a round

directly beside the bear about six inches from its paw, trying to scare it backwards. Without a second thought, I'd slammed the next round into the chamber ready to touch it off. For the big bears, often shoulders have to be broken down because even a heart shot can get you mauled to death because it can take a bit for the bear to realize it's dead. But if you take out both shoulders, they can't easily run over you.

The bear turned so fast it seemed a blur as it loped off down the hill. Just then I heard its cubs. I thought to myself "this is not good." Ally, not scared of the bear one bit, did freak out a little from the roar of the round going off over her head.

The bear then headed over to the neighbors through the forest. Their dogs all went nuts and I heard more shots being fired. I wondered, "did I mess up by not killing the bear and thinking we don't need cubs loose without their mum?" All I knew was, I was on guard because this could easily become a life and death issue and… I love life! Then I got a call with the news that one of my neighbors had been mauled really badly the day before and that bear was still on the loose. I wondered if this was the same bear that tore up my neighbor?

Part of the bear troubles were caused by some neighbors who had been careless with their trash. I hauled mine off daily because I just didn't want any problems. And, many kept freezers outside their cabins because their places were so small inside. My landlord did this and because I did not have my own freezer, I placed a few things in his. The bears had learned this was a picnic basket with a feast inside.

Later that night I stepped out to view the stars and to listen. I could hear the bears breaking brush and panting hard less than 75 yards away. It became very obvious they were in no hurry to leave. So when I crawled into my sleeping bag on top of my cot, I had my thunderstick laying on my chest with the zipper of the bag unzipped.

As I lay resting, I gave thanks for our protection and for the opportunity to live in Alaska. Bears are just one of the many reasons I love living here. It fills me with awe and wonder, and makes me feel so alive seeing all the great things the *Great Mystery* has made. I drifted off to sleep, not knowing what a long night it would turn out to be.

CHAPTER 10

They Lied!

After waking up I made an extra strong cup of coffee because I did not get to sleep until some time after 5:00 A.M. That brownie and her cubs kept trying to raid my home and the landlords because of the freezer full of goodies.

The Alaska State Troopers showed up at about 3:00 A.M. and they told me a bear removal team would be coming out that day. They lied! No one ever came even though we tried for many days to get some help. John lost most of his freezer food because they kept opening up the freezer, helping themselves to a feast. I only lost a little and found a new, safe place to store my food, using this as a life lesson. Don't ever keep a freezer outside your cabin, it can get you killed!

When I went outside, I could still hear them in the brush, so it appeared they weren't leaving and I could not blame them. After all, they had found free food. As I puttered around the cabin, I placed Ally back out on her run and watched her like a hawk. Often she ran loose, but since she had been upset all night, making a big ruckus off and on when the bears would be within two to three feet of my door as they circled, I knew she wanted them. Even though she always came when called, if off the cable run, I was not positive she would listen.

Needing a nap and because the bears seemed to be more active in the dark, I decided to sleep during the day. I would have to bring Ally in because this bear and her cubs started coming right up to my cabin's door which, I realized, was of little use since it was an interior door, not a solid door like most use on their cabins. This door was hollow. Not liking the feel of that fact, I decided it might be a good time to think about relocating to a cabin with a real door!

Ally and I both slept and I'm glad we did because that night the bears took it up a notch. I was able to watch them with ease because I was loaned some "night vision" (technology that provides users with some vision in total darkness and improved vision in low-light environments) that let me see their every move.

As day turned into night there was a lot of bear activity. They did not hit my home that night but they did my neighbors and their dogs were going nuts. I lost count of warning shots fired. At times I was able to watch them go through the trees and brush with the "night vision." It was quite fascinating, to say the least. In order to use this vision set, I had to have all my lights off so the bears could not watch me while I watched them.

Everyone for a couple of miles had started having trouble and it appeared it was not the same bears doing all the raiding. Nobody went outside without carrying a shotgun at all times since this is the firearm of choice for bear defence for many

They Lied!

Alaskans. Even though we liked the moose and hated to see so many of the calves eaten right away, several people started hoping the moose would start calving early so the bears would leave us alone. But, we were about two weeks out from the calving season.

Ally had started sleeping closer to me than she normally did and when I was up, she sat right next to my stool. She was on guard with ears at full attention every night and I gave her a lot more love and treats in her food bowl than she normally received. I felt so blessed to have her by my side. I was extremely dependent on her nose and ears for alerting me to what was going on around me.

CHAPTER 11

Guess Who's Back?

I went to bed at 5:00 A.M. and finally drifted off after an exciting night of a visit by the bears, along with sound effects! They were back in all their glory with the neighbor's dogs, as usual, going nuts. They had been leaving my home alone with the exception of pushing on my cabin's wall which really got my attention. To hear a thud and then look out the window to see a massive bear staring back through the window less than three feet away, well…. it has a tendency to drive the idea of rest miles from your mind.

Then all of a sudden, I heard a crash. Jumping up, I watched the freezer being thrown around. Next, they were off with a big bag of food and this wouldn't do so I grabbed my thunderstick and a light and out the door I went. The old mother bear went right by my window and the cubs scattered. I went just a few feet when the thought occured to me that it might be easier on my feet and skin if I was wearing more clothing and some boots.

Back in the cabin I dressed in a hurry and was soon joined by my neighbor who had just woke up and had gone outside to see the freezer in the wrong location and my cabin's lights on. He asked me, "why did you not kill that bear?" I explained that I decided that bear hunting bare is not the best way to be remembered by those who are not used to seeing large, albino white things frolic in the woods at night just wearing underwear.

We did try to find her but with no success. I took up bear guard sitting in my cabin with windows open while smothering myself in Avon bug dope. Then, while swatting at the

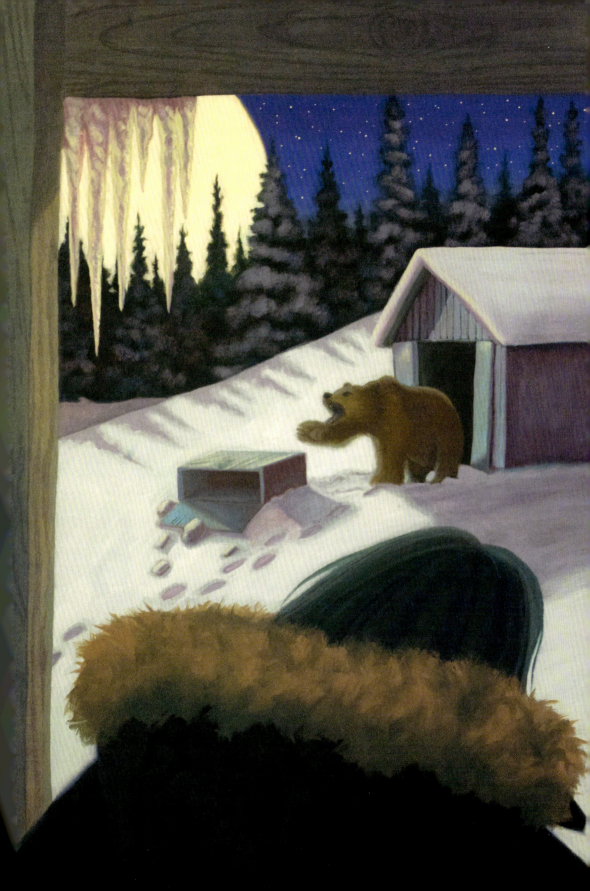

mosquitoes, I noticed the Northern Lights were starting to come on in a most spectacular way. I just had to laugh because they were some of the best I'd seen while on the Kenai and I couldn't really focus on them because I was trying to monitor those bears with the "night vision."

The three bears came back about sixty yards away, sitting in the alders, just watching my cabin and John's place, all the while making noises. John had left a light on and they did not seem to want to come in when lights were on. Then, with the Aurora's dancing, I was given the gift of listening to the bears talk. The cubs made the neatest little squeaks and grunts as they talked to each other and their mum. One could tell when they were not minding because their mum got on them at times for whatever they must have done wrong. They were rather fun to listen to as their little squeals reminded me of "come on, mum, let's go do it again," and their mum was saying, "wait until the lights go off."

After some time, one of the neighbor's dogs closed in on the bears and suddenly I heard its cries as they quickly killed it and ate it. This was part of the 'law' of the wild. Finally, they wandered off and I dozed off. By this point I was exhausted because this had been going on for several days.

    When I awoke, I ate a quick meal and loaded Ally in the truck for a little drive around the new road put in the previous year in order to check for fresh bear sign. Since Breakup had arrived and the snow was beginning to melt, the roads were starting to get frost heaves, turning to mush. This, however, left perfect conditions to see the tell-tale signs of the bears. In fact, I needed 4-wheel drive just to get through the roads.

    I saw more tracks than I could count from several different bears among which were the biggest tracks I had ever seen from some huge boar. My hat looked rather small inside its paw prints. I so hoped I got to see him to take his picture. Since bears, at times, are prone to be lazy, you can often find their tracks along dirt roads because it is much easer for them to trudge the road than to go overland.

    By the time the next day rolled around, I'd lost count of the days I'd been on my toes. The bears had come back after a while and Ally knew they were there. She kept going to the different walls of my cabin and listening as they circled my home. She stayed that way for a couple of hours with ears standing at attention. She would keep coming back, placing herself between me and the door, just standing there at attention. After a while they moved on and I dozed off. All of a sudden there was a horrific noise of breaking glass. Ally, "The Best Watch Dog In Alaska," was at the door going crazy. I bolted off my cot and grabbed the thunderstick. As I opened the cabin's door, into the woods the gangsters went. And although I could not see down the dark path, I knew where they were traveling so I started pumping 525-grain slugs down that path as fast as I could after them because their trying to open my cabin up was the last straw. I quickly reloaded and stood by, ready. I was not going into the dark to see what was going on, however, because that would be extremely dangerous.

The next day I tuned in to the local news on the radio and heard my friends, the bears, were in the news. There was a warning to people in my area concerning them because they were causing havoc enough to be considered extremely dangerous.

I ordered a special flashlight that was built into the forearm of a shotgun grip. I was not going to be in the position ever again of dealing with bears at night as I tried to fumble with a flashlight or my old headlamp while I worked a 12-guage for defense of life and property. I wanted to be able to see their rather large bodies as they rushed into the trees and be able to kill them. As I was to find out in future winters, that lighted forearm would come in very handy in protecting my dog team from angry moose, while on the trail, and dealing with wolves that fell alongside my team.

Much to my relief, that set of bears never bothered us again, but a few weeks later we moved to a more remote cabin that had a solid front door, and as it would turn out, an even bigger bear.

Guess Who's Back?

CHAPTER 12

An Explosion Of Life

After the countryside started to dry out in *the Moon When the Ice Goes Out of the Rivers*, "May," I heard of an old abandoned homestead as a possible place to relocate. It had been vacated for years and was well off the beaten path. After a long drive, I finally reached the mile long driveway that was strictly 4-wheel drive only and then just during the best of seasons.

As I slowly crawled along this road I was struck with a since of adventure, it felt like I had just parachuted into the thick of the Alaskan Bush. Suddenly, an old, two story cabin appeared in an opening, surrounded by a massive marshland with wide open views. Some old buildings were barely standing with their roofs sagging and their walls leaning outwards in ways that showed many a winter's snow had set heavily upon them.

Entering the cabin, the floor exploded with movement as squirrels and rodents scrambled for cover. There were piles of old pine cones, remnants that were almost as tall as I was that the squirrels had left. Obviously, this place had not been lived in for years.

A barrel woodstove was at the center of the large living room. At one end of this room was a kitchen area with ample room to cook and entertain large groups of friends. A stairway led upwards with a door leading into a side room. When I opened the door, it came alive with all kinds of creatures who were living in what had been, at one time, a library.

One of the creatures that made me jump was a Great Horned Owl, "Bubo virginianus." It flew so close to me as it left the room through the open ceiling, I could feel the wind off its wings. I stood in amazement as I mused, "how did all these critters manage to live with a bird of prey in the same room?" This room had a large skylight because the roof had caved in years before and was, for the most part, crushed flat against a floor that saged deeply from years of snow load. Interestingly, many of the books along the walls were still in good shape and would provide many hours of reading while I relaxed in the tranquility of the solitude of Alaska's Bush.

Climbing the stairs I found a large and very drafty room that was dry. Windows were all over the cabin which would make observations of the natural environment easy and as well natures observation of me also easy. I was very aware that nature is not God, but nature reveals Him. The hours I spent staring out the windows are treasured moments. There are 86,400 seconds in a day. Each, like a gold coin, once spent can never be regained. I still believe, as I did when moving into this remote, battered cabin, that the time spent observing the creations were well spent as I could see the fingerprints of the *Great Mystery* and His Son, Yiissus, the Christ.

Within the week I had shoveled out all the pine cones.

An Explosion Of Life

I soon realized the place was full of Wood Lemmings, "Myopus schisticolor." It took several days before I was able to figure out what this odd critter was. There are at least nine different kinds of lemmings throughout Alaska. Not finding anything that worked as a bait and not wanting to use a poison, they stayed with me, along with a few of the squirrels, as long as I lived there.

Each morning I would find squirrels running over my sleeping bag, some even sitting next to the alarm clock. I'd sneak a peak at them knowing that as soon as the clock sounded, they would scatter and chatter at the clock louder than the racket the old clock was making. I removed most of the squirrels.

As spring came alive, the marsh became an endless song as birds, and even frogs, joined in the chorus of the creation. I was reminded of the verse in the Biggest Book in Isaiah 55:12 which refers to the creation giving praise to Ellam Yua, "God the Father." It is written this way, "For you shall go out in joy and be led forth in peace; the mountains and the hills before you shall break forth into singing, and all the trees of the field shall clap their hands."

Soon one of the creations that the *Great Mystery* designed, and which I care very little for, came out in mass numbers.

An Explosion Of Life

CHAPTER 13

Tiny Tormentors

Yep… it was the Mosquito! Soon I had to wear a mosquito net on my head at all times when I was up and away from my cot.

I soon learned the inside of the old cabin was not much better than the outside, as far as mosquito control was concerned. Even though way off the beaten path, at one time a power line had been run to this homestead. I contacted the power company to see if service could be restored. I had devised a plan of attack against this enemy of Ally's and mine by which we were now being tormented.

Within days I was able to turn on a light bulb so off to town I went in search of a mosquito zapper. The box gave it a rating capacity to clear these pests for one square acre of land (43,560 square feet). Soon it was hanging upstairs close to my cot which by this time was covered with a hanging, mosquito net so I could hopefully get some sleep. I'd awake and at times the net would be so loaded with mosquitos that the new day's light was seriously dimmed. Ally insisted on sleeping under the net as well and soon learned that the cans of Avon-Skin-So-Soft Bug Guard insect repellent wasn't something she minded at all.

In short order the zapper started sparking as endless mosquitoes came to their end. For over five weeks the zapper seemed to be almost constantly buzzing as a pile of the dead critters stacked to over two feet in height and almost four feet in diameter. Eventually it became possible to live in the cabin without a head net on at all times, as long as I wore bug repellent, and although at times I heard the zapper, it wasn't one constant noise.

Tiny Tormentors

Ally and I would often sit next to the marsh in the best mosquito protection we could muster and watch moose and their calves browse. Every once in a while a big bull moose would come through. One of our favorites in the marsh was the Sandhill Cranes, "Grus canadensis," a rather large bird that has the most unmistakable call. I would describe it as something between an old squeaky shed door and maybe a French horn. I learned they are good to eat.

One evening I noticed a coyote, "Canis latrans," stalking slowly toward these young crane's nest after their chicks had hatched. All of a sudden the breeding pair started making a ruckus that let the coyote know it had been spotted. Within a short time both adult cranes were marching toward the coyote who now seemed quite unsure of itself. The cranes split and came in after this poor coyote with a ferocity I've rarely seen. Between jumping up and down, flying, and charging in together, they began to pluck the coyotes pelt to pieces as it yelped and tried to dart this way and that. The cranes most definitely had the upper hand. The attack continued a couple of minutes until the coyote bolted and fled for his life. The Sandhills charged after him and only when he had left the marsh did they return to their nest. I never saw him again.

The cabin windows were made up of many small window panes. Often the wind would blow through some of the gaps between the panes which was one of the main thoroughfares the mosquitos used to get inside. Although I loved seeing the view through them, all of a sudden I decided they seemed a little whimpy with that bear roaming the woods. Yep, I had a solid door but the windows would sometimes make a tinkling sound with the strong winds. It was inside these windows that my next adrenalin rush took place a few days later.

CHAPTER 14

His Eyes Are On Me

It was a quiet, cool night. I had built a fire in the woodstove and found a good book from the caved in library to go along with my cup of tea. Ally was napping in front of the stove and her snoring told me she was really out of it. No reading light was needed since it was still so bright outside. It was during *the Moon of Making Fat*, "June," and it really does not get dark. This month is so named because this is when food starts to become plentiful and the animals start gaining back the weight they lost the winter before.

His Eyes Are On Me

I had been enjoying my reading when I had the sensation I was being watched. The hair on the back of my neck stood up. Slowly looking up, I saw the biggest bear I had ever seen standing on his back legs peering down at me through those old windows. He was standing well over nine feet tall. I later took a tape measure to confirm his heighth. He just stood there staring, his eyes boring holes through my body. I have no way of knowing just how long we stared at each other, but it felt like hours. Then I reacted, having no memory of what I did next.

This bear was about twelve feet from me. The base of the stairway was about eight feet toward him. All I know is that one moment I'm locking eyes with this bear and the next I'm at the top of the stairs with my thunderstick in hand, yelling for Ally, who is still snoring, to get herself upstairs.

I do not remember running toward the bear as I apparently leaped over my clueless, best friend, as I bolted up the stairs. I do not remember crossing the bedroom and taking down the 12-guage. I just know one moment I was sitting locking eyes with the bear and the next moment I was at the top of the stairs where I knew that if it came through the window, I'd stand my best chance to tackle this monster.

As Ally made her way up the stairs with a look of annoyance, I was never so glad to see her. It must have dawned on her that something was wrong for she quickly came to attention. I tried to see this bear from upstairs but with no success. Finally, ever so slowly, I creeped down the stairs, ready for the bear in the best manner I could think of only to find, much to my relief, it was gone. I was unable to spot it from the house but decided to stay inside until morning. I was not even tempted to sleep!

Without any headlamp, I sat up the long hours of the night keeping watch. To entertain myself, I planned the kind of cabin I would construct someday that would have bears in mind. Little did I realize this bear was far from being through with me.

In the month called *the Woodcutter's Moon*, "August," I came back to the cabin late one morning. I parked the Bronco, headed toward the cabin, which I unlocked, and let Ally go inside. I placed my thunderstick against the inside wall and went to retrieve the groceries I had just purchased when the brush exploded close to the cabin. The breeze had been gently blowing toward the brush so Ally had not caught the two bears scent. A large, sow Brown Bear was being followed by the large, boar Brown bear I'd seen hanging around the cabin. I was in a bad position but they did not even seem to notice me as they passed just a few feet away. I knew now there were two bears in the neighborhood.

I did not see the sow ever again but a few days later, this boar charged me as I got out of my truck. Swinging around I prepared to take him on as I backed up toward the house. He broke his charge off as I opened the cabin door. Ally and I went into the cabin but we did so with Ally trying to make a stand. I had to grab her collar and drag her inside. He was such a beautiful bear that I can still see his fur shimmering in the light of that afternoon.

His Eyes Are On Me

CHAPTER 15

The Gentle Prompting

I had so enjoyed that summer, spending endless hours fishing for salmon on the Kenai and Kasilof rivers. Because I did not have a freezer to keep them in and had not taken up canning yet, I would just catch what Ally and I could share for a meal or two and be done with the catching. Then I would resort to what I would call not-fishing-fishing. I would remove my hook, making sure the weight I was using was still attached, and place a piece of red, yellow, or orange yarn on it. Then I would resume casting as I talked to friends who were fishing, the *Great Mystery*, or just stay lost in my thoughts. When doing this with friends, they were never aware of what I was doing. I just enjoyed the fellowship and the creation. Later at the coffee shop, as they kidded me, I'd hear the stories about how I was the worst fisherman they had ever seen. I'd just smile and think, "if you only knew."

That first season on the Kenai Peninsula I learned a lot from my friend, Larry Vally, on how to fish for salmon. I owe this man much gratitude because he taught lessons on fishing that has continued to help feed me. We spent many an hour fishing, talking, and as an Elder, he instructed me on the proper way to live. It reminds me of what it says in the Biggest Book in Proverbs, chapter four. I still feel blessed for this mans input into my life.

With winter approaching and realizing I could not keep the road open and traveling in and out would have to be on foot, I decided to move north toward the end of the road system on the western side of the Kenai. At that time I was not ready for a dog team.

So, in *the Moon of Falling Leaves*, "October," toward the

end of the month, I packed up and moved to one of the most creative homes I'd ever seen – a large, rectangular water tank. Its walls bulged out because one winter it had not been drained before it had frozen. A door had been made into its side with a cutting torch and a roof built on top.

It was located in a place most people would not consider, let alone dream of living because it was, for the most part, somewhere between a salvage yard and an obstacle course that was surrounded by a spruce forest. The man who owned the place just wanted somebody to live there to keep an eye on things. No rent was necessary. It was a great place… unless the heater failed, and would definitely be bear proof, but it held its own danger that came close to costing me my life!

One of the most peculiar objects in the "yard" was a fiberglass building that had been used on the oil platforms in Cook Inlet that would later become my home, after I had it relocated.

At this new place, where I planned to live only for the upcoming winter, I found squirrels had been living there. They had chewed their way through the eves just under the roof and I would have a long fight trying to rid myself of them. They chewed their way through my food containers, tried to nest in my clothing, and sat on the sparce furnishings as they would chatter at me. Nothing was safe from their rentless chewing of anything that caught their fancy.

It did not take long and I had the corner filled with my few possessions. The place was heated by an old natural gas furnace that hung from the ceiling. It looked a lot like those I had seen in many a service station hanging in the bays where they did maintenance on vehicles. I flipped the switch and it started up. I set the thermometer to a level to take off the chill because a strong, cold breeze had begun to blow, carrying a few snowflakes with it, the first of the year.

I started unpacking and realized I was just tired. Why, I did not know, I'd had plenty of sleep the night before. The more I unpacked and put things away, the more tired I became. I had a dull but throbbing headache and decided to go to bed. I looked out the door and saw a few inches of snow already drifting up beside the tank along with a fierce wind that was now bending the trees. It was difficult to see much, even with the headlamp, because we were close to a whiteout, a term used

The Gentle Prompting

when there is so much snow flying in the air you can see nothing but white. Under these conditions, I was glad I was not on the road but at the tank, especially with the way I was feeling.

I headed toward my cot and was going to crawl in when I felt compelled to spend a moment getting the smoke detector out and hung up. But I sat and argued with myself that I could do it the next day. Then, this thought came to me, "If my Mum asks me if I put my smoke detector up before my first sleep," as I knew she would, I didn't want to tell her, "I did not!" And although I was well into my years, I still to this day wanted to show honor and respect to my Mum. So, I got up and found the box with the fire extinguishers, smoke detectors, and carbon monoxide detector in it.

With the smoke detector hung with new batteries, I decided to put a new battery into the carbon monoxide detector. I then set it close to the floor below the level of the bed. Because carbon monoxide is a heavy gas, a detector must always be kept below the level at which a person is sleeping. All of a sudden it started screaming with the meter showing the level of carbon monoxide climbing toward what seemed to me to be a very high level. I thought, "this has to be wrong" and so I pulled the battery, reinserting it once more. Within seconds the scenerio repeated itself and then it dawned on me that the reason I was so tired and my head was hurting so badly was all due to carbon monoxide poisoning. The furnace was faulty.

I opened the door and shut down the furnace. Standing in the cold wind I felt a little better. A couple of small windows had been cut into the side of the water tank. I opened them and let the breeze blow in. After about a half hour, I closed it all and started up the furnace to see if I could just warm it up a little and then shut it off before the carbon monoxide level became too dangerous. Within a very short time the meter started screaming and all had to be shut down and the windows and door opened again.

By this time there was no way I could see to drive somewhere else for the night because I was in a total whiteout. So, after the room cleared of the poison, I closed off all but one window, shut the gas off to the furnace, and crawled into my sleeping bag, still feeling sick.

The next day I felt worse so locking in my four-wheel

drive, I headed for medical help. I was told that the levels I reported on the detector were so high that if I had gone to sleep, I would not have woke up because I would have died in my sleep. I was sick for several days and stayed with a friend. A new furnace was put in and there were no more problems.

As I lay that long night for the first time inside the water tank, even though I was sick, I had more gratitude than I could express in words to Yeshua Ha-Mashiach, "Jesus The Christ." For it was His prompting to put up my detectors that kept me alive. He brought to my mind Proverbs 1:8-9 which says this, "Hear, my son, your father's instruction, and forsake not your mother's teaching, for they are a graceful garland for your head and pendants for your neck." Now, I had not been raised by a dad, he had moved away when I was a boy. But my Mum had brought me up with instructions and teachings. One of them had been "always play it safe and put up needed protection such as smoke and carbon monoxide detectors." If I had not followed her instruction, I'd not be here to type these words. So here is a clear, down to earth example of what it means and a life story that is based on reading Proverbs 1:8-9. And to this day, I always follow this instruction.

The Gentle Prompting

CHAPTER 16

The "Dog House"

I spent that winter reading books on trapping. I bought some cross country skis and checked out the trails and country side. I spent hours writing poetry, something I'd done for years. I met every few days with friends for coffee and started planning the construction of my 'new' house I'd start building that coming spring. There was small game hunting, ice fishing, and animal watching.

The "Dog House"

The most enjoyable event that winter was watching the fox family that lived inside the pile of pipes next to the water tank. I had the odd moose come through but had no problems with any of them. I showed them respect and gave them their distance. They'd look at me as I'd sit on the sunny days on the little covered porch drinking coffee, watching them and the birds that would come to the bird and suet feeders (a cake of hard fat mixed with seeds, grains, nuts and fruit that is used as food for backyard and wild birds).

One day that spring, while sitting on the porch, much to my surprise I noticed the two foxes I'd been watching all winter were both sitting on top of the pile of pipes. The male fox, which can be called correctly by four different names: dog, dog fox, tod, or reynard, was at one end of the pile of pipes while the female fox, called a vixen, was at the other end of the pipe. And there, running in and out of the pile of pipes, were the young fox's known as either kits, cubs, or pups.

They played right in front of Ally who just sat there with me as we watched for the next hour or so. The vixen and the dog would at times give us a glance as we were scarcely 30

The "Dog House"

yards away, but they did not seem slightly concerned about our presence. They had observed us all winter and as we had given them their space, they had become accustomed to us being there. I was never able to know for sure how many kits there were because they were never all in one big pile in the open. My best guess was at least five.

As Breakup unfolded completely, the odd bear would ramble through the yard. Moose caves learned to browse on some of the alder bushes. Because suet is a tasty treat for bears and I did not want them on the porch, I put that feeder away until the upcoming winter.

I then started working on the fiberglass building I was to name the "Dog House," a little building just under twelve feet long and eight feet wide. When standing inside I could just place my fist between my head and the ceiling. It was built for water tight construction so the two doors were like hatches on a ship because it had been barged out to oil platforms where it would be hoisted aboard.

Everything had been stripped from the little building. I had desired my own home and nothing big was needed.

The "Dog House"

I asked the owner of the property what he would take for the building and he said, "if you can get it moved, it's yours, I just want it gone." So I started a remodel in earnest.

The walls were only two inches thick with no insulation so it was apparent a good heat source was needed. I ordered a small wood cookstove complete with a warming rack and a tank to heat water that would attach to its side.

There were three windows and since this building had been built for safety reasons to withstand a broken cable flying through the air, all windows were bullet proof. Bears could not easily open it up.

Four holes in the ceiling, where air conditioning units had been, were covered with plexiglass (a see through, almost unbreakable 'plastic'). Through them I could view the Northern Lights. Inside there was a counter with deep stainless steel shelves built in that had doors. I put in two small kitchen sinks and a small refrigerator went underneath one end of the counter. I installed a small propane two burner range that had a small oven. Two propane lights were plumbed onto the walls to give light.

The "Dog House"

A bed was built high enough off the floor that large storage containers could be stored beneath. A latch was built into the top of the bed so it could be lifted up to get to the compartments where clothing was stored. It was similar to what many sailors have on a ships berth (a shelf like sleeping space). Above the bed was a full length shelf and under it I built a fishing pole rack for all my fishing poles. On the back wall between the bed and upper shelf, I built an archery rack to hang my compound bow.

Next to the bed I built a gun cabinet and next to that a shelf system that had a table that folded up in place for use, folding down when not needed. I added minimal wiring. I picked up a high back office chair, the only furniture, and added a heat shield that was placed in the corner behind the wood cookstove that was plumbed through the flat roof. After a few days of diligent work it was finished, ready to be moved but to where? I had no money to buy property.

I took the matter of moving this building and a piece of land upon which to move it in prayer to the *Great Mystery*. Within days my prayer was to be answered when a friend's friend

The "Dog House"

heard that I was looking for a place to set the little building in Kasilof, a small town with a population of 777. All buildings in the area, including homes, consisted of two churches, a post office, museum, a general store combined with a restaurant, a gas station-store combination, the fire station, and a school. Some drive through it without realizing they have just passed through a small community.

There were several mushers in the community and a trail system leading into the Caribou Hills that was wonderful for mushing. It is also the home of the T-200 Dog Sled Race, one of the qualifers for both the Yukon Quest and the Iditarod. I figured this was the place to set up a dog yard.

There was a piece of land with just over six acres that needed somebody around to keep an eye on it. If I would agree to move there, I could live there as long as I wanted for just watching over things. Electricity was on the property and the gravel road going out to it was kept plowed.

I loaded up Ally and went to investigate. A large lake for trout fishing was within a half mile. Moose, bear, Lynx, "Lynx canadensis," and other critter's tracks were all over the

The "Dog House"

place. And, it had all the room I needed for a dog yard. All I needed now was to have the building moved, dig a hole for the outhouse, build the outhouse and I'd be set. I found a local building mover and within a few days Ally and I were sleeping for the first time in the big "Dog House" in Kasilof, Alaska. The place was quiet and it felt good to be living in something I owned and even though it was small, I felt blessed.

I could manage to have three friends over at once. One would sit on the bed but would have to sit forward since the shelf above prevented him from sitting up straight. One would get the chair. One could sit on the counter and one would stand. Then every fifteen minutes we would rotate to the next position. Needless to say, I did not entertain company very often.

The "Dog House"

CHAPTER 17

More Hard Earned Wisdom

Soon it was the season of *the Red Salmon Time Moon*, "July," and living about 15 minutes from Cook Inlet, I fished and beach combed. I also started hiking deep into the mountains. I explored old gold mines, taking road trips way into the Interior where I encountered many very interesting Bush Rats who shared tales that kept me riveted to my seat.

Soon fall was upon me and the termination dust was covering the mountain tops. Termination dust is the first dusting of snow that signals winter is on its way. The world broke forth in vibrant colors as the *Great Mystery* took His paint palet and with brush strokes turned the country into a mosaic too beautiful for words.

Soon geese, swans, and the Sandhill Cranes could be heard flying south along with flocks of ducks. One could listen to the bull moose starting to call as they challenged each other into fierce battles over the herds of cow moose they maintained.

As the temperatures dropped, at times I'd see the Snowshoe Hare, Rock Ptarmigan, and Ermine, "Mustela erminea," already turning white as their winter camouflage set in. I felt sorry for them since there wasn't much snow yet and they really started to stand out after losing their summer colors.

During this time I realized I had a problem with heating the "Dog House." I had put in the wood cookstove, not thinking just how small the firebox was. With the spruce wood I had to burn, I could go about two hours before needing to reload the firebox. Since I had no insulation in the walls and a one-half inch plate of steel in the floor, the place would soon get very cool.

As winter progressed I'd wake to temperatures below zero degrees, unless I set an alarm and got up every hour to hour and a half to reload the stove. Doing this for days on end soon brought on utter exhaustion.

Wanting to get some sleep, I ordered an oil-drip stove from Fairbanks. This was the same type of stove I'd used while living in Fairbanks to heat my cabin when the temperatures dipped down to over fifty degrees below zero. I had always stayed warm. It required no electricity, which is the way I needed to have it at my cabin in the Bush. Although there was power at this location, it would frequently be out due to a problem somewhere.

Much to my disappointment, when the stove arrived at the post office, it had been crushed in shipping. I filed all the paper work, since it was insured, and talked to the store in Fairbanks that had shipped it to me. They told me they would in no way send me another one until they received their money from the post office for their damaged stove for which I had paid.

I had put together a fifty-five gallon oil drum on a metal stand, which was way more than I needed, to feed the stove that I was sure would do a fine job heating such a small place. As the temperatures dropped and I waited for my stove, I decided to stay with a friend for a few days to get some rest.

When I stopped by the "Dog House" to check things out, it appeared someone had been there because there were fresh tracks in the snow. I decided to stay for the night, and after a couple of hours of running the woodstove wide open, the temperature finally reached the low seventies.

I needed to eat some dinner and since all my canned food was frozen, the only easy choice was the peanut butter which, placed next to the stove, was starting to thaw. I decided to have a peanut butter sandwich so I took two frozen slices of bread and threw them on top of my woodstove to thaw out.

After this mission was completed, with some work I managed to get one very large spoonful of peanut butter on a very cold spoon from the silverware drawer, which was not so bad as long as I left my wool mittens on. After smearing the peanut butter on the bread, I plopped the spoon in my mouth to lick off the peanut butter and had the bottom of the spoon stick hard to my wet tongue! That's right, just like licking an ice tray. It did not want to come off and there was no water that was not frozen solid that I could use to try to loosen it. I had to start breathing hard through my mouth with my face over the woodstove before the spoon would come free. To say the least, I lost my ability to taste very much for several days and my tongue felt like it had been slammed in a trunk lid. This was truly an Alaskan experience I care not to repeat. Note to self: don't lick frozen spoons!

I knew I had a problem when I came home and found all my canned goods that I had stuck inside the refrigerator to keep from freezing, frozen solid. It makes one smile when you have to stick your hands in your refrigerator or freezer to warm them up. I usually just laugh, since most people have never experienced some of the joys of living in the Bush. Most of my canned goods had frozen and both ends had bulged out. I told an old Bush Rat what had happened and was told that when you know you're going to leave and all will freeze up, place all canned goods on their sides and they won't bulge out. I looked at him with a look of disbelief and he just smiled and said, "I know you think I'm feeding you a line, but just try it." So the next time I left, knowing I would get frozen out, I did as suggested and upon return found all my canned goods in good shape. Who would have thunk?

Things like the propane that keeps your fridge, lights and cookstove running just freeze up at about 42 degrees below zero. You have to bring the propane tank in to let it warm up so it will start flowing again. You never set it close to the wood or oil drip stove to thaw out because this can be dangerous.

Because the cold is such a problem, I actually ran all my propane lines on the inside of my cabin's walls just to try to get around this problem of freezing. I also found that lamp oil freezes up. One needs to use kerosene fuel if your cabin is not always going to be kept warm.

Drinking water becomes more of a problem because the jugs freeze and break. You need more of them in the winter since you have to put less water in each of them so when frozen, they stay in the shape most useful, you know… with the bottom still in them. You try to keep one of them with you in the truck on the floor next to the heater so when you get home you have drinking and dish water. Once you are home, you keep the jug that was in your truck as high as you can in your cabin so the heat from your stove will keep the water from freezing because cabin floors often stay very cold.

As that long night rolled on, the sound of trash cans being banged around came from the neighbors. Because my only close neighbor was often gone and he did not keep trash put away as it should be, that local Brown Bear that patroled this area was causing all the racket.

I watched Ally for a long time as she sniffed the air and listened to something that I could not hear on the backside of my homestead. I checked later and found huge tracks from that bear. He used the back woods behind my house as his trail both coming and going as he feasted on trash can stew. I'd been hearing reports of bears still being in the area and was wondering when they would choose to den up since the lake next to my house had already frozen to the depth of six inches over the past few days. This signals the start of ice-fishing season, something a lot of us do to help put food in our homes.

One of the oddest sounds that I have ever heard was the sound I've come to love, the sound of the ice when it is freezing hard. It is loud and rather a foreboding sound that would be unnerving if you were not aware what was making it. The first time I heard it I could not place it with anything I'd ever heard before. I've likened it to the water giving thanks to Ellam Yua for yet another beautiful year in the creation He made way back in Deep Time (in the beginning). When one gets to add Northern Lights to this music from nature, it is especially beautiful! Ally seemed to thrive in this cold as she just laid out in the snow under the Northern Lights and guarded her best friend - me.

Finally in *the Moon of the Popping Trees*, "December," my new stove arrived. At last I'd be warm. The day it arrived I had the wood cookstove pulled out and placed into storage for future use. The new oil-drip stove from Fairbanks easily went in and soon the stove came alive. I'd now have a very warm home with this heater on its lowest setting. In fact, the temperature had been staying around the 80-degree range and although hotter than I liked, it felt like such a treat. It was always warm inside the "Dog House" because it burned right around the clock. Every night I'd bring home 5 gallons of diesel and dump it into my oil drum. I kept this up until my drum was full and then once a month start the process all over again.

As the temperature dropped way down into the negative numbers, I was hoping the floor wouldn't get so cold that it hurt to walk on it. It is also kind of wearying to have your house temperature up in the "I think if it gets any hotter in here I will burst into flames range," and still be able to put food items on the inside floor to keep them frozen, if you so desired. I had experienced many a time when at fifty below zero, several inches of frost would be about a foot high on the inside cabin walls, all the while I thought my flesh was going to melt off my bones and freeze in puddles on my living room floor. Would this "Dog House" be any better since it had a half inch plate of steel under the fiberglass that covered the floor? I was soon to find out.

More Hard Earned Wisdom

CHAPTER 18

Beyond Belief

As the temperatures plummeted, I woke one night covered in sweat. I unzipped my sleeping bag and decided I'd open the door to let things cool off a little. Sweat covered the bottom of my feet and as soon as they touched the floor, they froze to it, much like licking an ice tray with a wet tongue. I yanked my feet up as I tried to get back on my bed and promptly ripped much of the skin off the bottom of both feet.

The next day I bought a very nice rug so when I got up, I could stand on it and get into my sheep skin slippers. My feet hurt for days and it was very uncomfortable to walk. Once Ally found I had the rug, she decided she'd rather sleep inside on it rather than in the snow bank I thought she had preferred. I now realized the snow bank was warmer than the floor. Oh, how wrong I had been and I felt really bad for this obvious blunder.

Dog teams started coming by my place towing four-wheelers. The mushers had little snow and they needed to get the teams in shape for the winter. I soon fell in love with the sound of the neighbor's teams when they would start singing to each other. I was so looking forward to having my place set up for a dog team.

Because I knew almost nothing about mushing, I decided the best way to get into this lifestyle was to join a mushing club and volunteer to take care of teams when their mushers went on vacation. I joined the local mushing club and soon found myself riding a snowmobile because the trails needed grooming (packed down and smoothed out). Moose often walk the trails and leave deep tracks. If a team runs into such during a race it is very possible for a dog to step into a track and break its leg. So before every race, the holes get filled in and the trail smoothed out by a snowmobile pulling a trail groomer. After a new snowstorm, one also needs to groom and pack down the trail.

Every once in a while I'd get to be near the dogs as I watched them put into their harness and attached to the gangline (a central line connecting a sled, etc. to the individual tuglines of the animals that pull it). There are three ways to mush dogs. The "Siwash" technique, which is the way most mushers run today, has dogs running in two's all in a row, one on either side of the gangline in behind the leader or leaders.

Eskimo peoples in the far north mush their dogs with the "Fan Hitch" technique since they do not have trees, bushes, and the like to deal with. This lets each dog work its way through the snow and ice in front of it.

The third technique is called "Traditional." It is not common these days except for those who live deep in the Bush who have to put in their trails with snowshoes. I now mush my dogs only traditional and each dog runs between two lines to which their harness is attached.

Beyond Belief

I had been watching the dogs being hooked up for just a little while when someone discovered I could operate a grill. At some of these events hot dogs and hamburgers are sold. So one Saturday, while I was wearing an apron and grilling away, someone called my name. "Hey, Bill! the next musher up for this short sprint is not going to make it so you are going to mush his team!" I said, "you've got to be kidding, I don't know how to mush!"

As they were taking off my apron and placing the racing jersey over me while dragging me toward the waiting sled, I was told "don't worry!" Phil Hookman told me, "when you see my arm come down, you yell 'hike' as loud as you can and don't let go, the dogs know the trail!" All of a sudden I was standing on the sled runners, very concerned, and Phil's arm dropped down so I screamed, "hike!"

The dogs went from making a very loud ruckus and lunging all over the place to totally quite as we launched like a cruise missle. As we hit the first corner I almost fell off and someone yelled, "squat down!" I did. The dogs picked up more speed and I prayed really hard. I had never zipped through trees so fast and after what seemed like an eternity I saw the finish line, much to my relief!

As I crossed the finish line they yelled, "slow down" and I yelled back, "I don't know how!" They said, "put your foot on the brake," and I screamed, "what brake?" Some mushers intercepted the dogs and after being drug along, got us slowed down. In all fairness, I'd never been close to a dog sled. I did not know they had brakes. When I had approached the sled, I had not been looking down but with trepedition was looking up at the dogs that were going berserk and the starting line.

Somehow I managed to get 4th that day out of a whole passel of mushers. Not bad for a guy who had never touched a dog sled before. I truly believe the only reason I did so well was because I did not know I had a brake because if I had known, I'd have been riding it most of the way! That was my first race and likely my last race because I just don't enjoy that kind of adrenalin rush.

A photo was taken as I crossed the finish line and I was beside myself with excitement. I was beyond hooked, I was going to have my own team by the following winter as sure

Beyond Belief

as the *Great Mystery* had made little green apples. So I started filling in for mushers who went on vacations and would never have believed that one of the teams I took care of several times would become mine after their musher passed away. All I could think about was dogs, sleds, and anything to do with mushing. I read anything and everything I could on the subject.

Beyond Belief

CHAPTER 19

Almost Too Good To Be True

Since it was already *the Moon When the Ice Goes Out of the Rivers*, "May," and bear problems were starting, I started thinking that a new place to set the "Dog House" was in order. Besides, it would be nicer to be closer to the mushing trails. Even though owning my own team was a while away, I took the matter before the *Great Mystery*.

One day, a close friend informed me they wanted to build a cabin in Alaska for a place to vacation whenever they were in a traveling mood. Would I find them a remote property and help build it? They would supply all the construction costs, I could earn a little money, and then move onto the property as the caretaker for as many years as I liked. And, oh yes, a dog yard would be just fine.

Because I wore leg braces due to the vehicle that ran over me while working in the Lower-49 as a Land Surveyor, and having both my shoulders rebuilt, and having been retired from the military after being crushed by some big, heavy equipment, I was not on the top of anyones list to hire as an employee. Consequently, I had done any odd jobs I could find to make ends meet such as painting houses, being a Mr. Fixit man, trapping, cutting firewood, and the like. I was able to work, I was just slower than many and had to take more breaks than most. So, a chance to make the money to get me through the winter with the added bonus of a place to move my little "Dog House" was a winning combination. I started looking in earnest over remote property, sending my friend all the info I collected.

Within a few weeks some property, off the beaten path, was purchased in Kasilof, and the work began. I picked a high point, removing enough trees to put in a driveway and parking area. I then dropped and removed trees where the cabin would sit, branching and stacking all the trees for future firewood. Not much happened for a while since the ground was too frozen for the contractor to put in the driveway or clear out all stumps and brush piles where the cabin would sit. The "Dog House" could not be moved onto the property until all the ground work was done. Thawing was also needed before the six foot holes could be dug for all 15 of the sonotubes (a cardboard tube used as the form when pouring concrete columns) that would support the cabin that would be approximately four feet off the ground.

Low bush cranberries meant there would be plenty to put up for jam. A moose and really cute newborn calf had come through the building pad area. A tree on the hill next to the house had a bald eagles, "Haliaeetus leucocephalus," nest so quite often I'd watch them while they would roost. In the evening I could hear the Loons, "Gavia immer," make their most beautiful call off the nearby lake. It appeared I was moving to the right place.

By the middle of *the Moon of Making Fat*, "June," all needed brush and stumps had been removed, the driveway and parking area were in, and the spot for the cabin cleared.

I made a large concrete slab for stacking firewood and a smaller one for my propane tank. I put Ally's name on the smaller slab along with her paw print and on the large pad I put my name and the date.

Then I started framing (the action, method, or process of constructing, making or shaping something) the cabin. Big utility trucks delivered all the building materials at once.

Next, my little, blue "Dog House" was delivered and set right where I wanted it. I was home. It felt good but boy, there was a lot of work to complete before winter set in.

To relax, I started walking a 2.6 mile path on a dead-end road and then looped back. On the second day out, I noticed a bear had walked the same path, leaving fresh piles on the road. Because I always walked with Ally off her leash and packed a thunderstick when we were out, I was not fearful but kept on guard. If you train yourself to look deep rather than most who just see the trees, you will have the privilege of seeing all kinds of wonderful critters. Since Ally was extremely alert, this gave me a great sense of what was going on around me.

About a fourth mile from the cabin, a Brown Bear killed a moose calf in one of my friends back yard and tore up the cow. I worried it was the cow and calf moose that had been staying close to my place. I was glad to see her and the calf show up a few days later, greatly relieved it was not my moose that had been munched.

Before I started building on the cabin I prayed to the Father, as I always do when working on a job. I asked Him for protection, success with the construction, a lot of wisdom, and to make the materials stretch. I was truly overwhelmed with gratitude because He had chosen to give me this opportunity.

I started building the cabin. Since I was not a carpenter by trade but had helped many others with their projects, I was eager to implement some ideas as to how it should be built. I had seen homes in Fairbanks with walls that were one foot thick so I decided to build the same. Before long I had 12 inches of insulation in the walls, floor, and ceiling and then things got crazy!

The cow and her calf came through where I had Ally staked out and the moose somehow got tangled in the half inch stainless cable I used for my dog run which ran just over six feet off the ground between two trees. This resulted in the removal of piles of the moose's hair as it was pulled out. I saved some of it for fly tying. Ally, I thought, made it through unharmed and I figured the experience would put a bad taste in the cows mind for my homestead and she might avoid it. WRONG! This brought up my latest, truly Alaskan experience.

I took a walk into the woods on the property to sit beneath my favorite tree to cool down. While sitting on a log with my glass of sun tea, the cow, with her newborn, came out of the bushes with a whole lot of attitude. That's right! And she was less than 15 feet away with her hackles up. I had brought the 12-guage but I was taken off guard and unable to back away. I aimed for the middle of her chest while talking quietly to her about the negative consequences that were about to unfold for us both if she came any closer. I am very grateful she decided to turn around and leave me. I knew she could bring her leg foward with a hard kick and it would not go well for me. I never took a nap under that tree again.

CHAPTER 20

The Forest Fire

A forest fire started in the next water drainage over, growing in no time at all to over 20,000 acres, which is about 31.5 square miles. The plume (a large quantity of smoke, dust, fire, or water that rises into the air in a column) off this fire was at 40,000 feet, which is something like 7.5 miles high. Then ash started raining all over me.

As the fire drew closer the fire fighters started throwing everything they could at it with little to no success. Many

The Forest Fire

cabins were burned and most people were evacuated for saftey. As I framed the floor, first story walls and ceiling of the first story, I was told if I stacked the building materials under the cabin, which was about four feet off the ground, I would have a smaller area to defend. The fire fighters might try to save my project as the fire steadily marched toward me, showing no sign it was going to slow down.

I worked around the clock to finish moving all the lumber, then started cutting out more trees and brush. I was giving it my best shot at making a defendable barrier, especially since the winds were supposed to reach 30 plus miles an hour that coming weekend. I was hoping that badly needed rain would show up soon, and I earnestly prayed for it, especially after a fire fighter told me the night before flames were over 500 feet high.

The smoke in the air around the cabin looked like fog at times, burning my eyes and nose. Looking toward the heavens the sky looked like what I am guessing Hell might appear, a rolling mass of indescribable action, fiery, and death all rolled into one massive violent view that all but overtakes ones

visual senses. Just the look of this made me think a person might really want to consider where they are going to spend eternity and get things right while there is still time! It says in the Biggest Book in Matthew 24:27-51 that we will not know the hour of the end and the conquences will be severe for those who are not ready!

With the forest fire driving out the animals, seven Brown Bears had to be shot in defense of life and property. This was sad but I understood. I suspected there would be even more as the infurno roared away.

Before long the fire had burned over 50 thousand acres (78 square miles). It was one big fire. I drove to the town of Sterling to buy a brush hog (a powered machine that uses a rotating blade or blades to cut vegetation) because I needed to get a nice firebreak (an area of land that has had plants and trees removed to stop the spread of a fire) as fast as I could.

The Kenai has the largest beetle kill forest in North America. These dead and dying white and black spruce are easily ignited. On the property on which I'd started building, most of the trees were still healthy, but some were not so fortunate.

The Forest Fire

For many people, insurance was not an option because they were so far out of a fire fighting district they could not get coverage. And, most do not have wells to supply the water needed to fight a fire. The property I was building on was within the 5-mile radius required for insurance purposes and the new fire station being built was almost ready for the equipment and crew to move in.

As that week wore on, and on account of the fires, I was a tree dropping, brush removing, wood stacking madman. Before long the fire was only seven to eight miles away. That seems like a lot of miles, but with it covering over 55,000 acres in less than three days, you can see how fast this fire moved. Then the *Great Mystery* sent a blessing and it started raining which helped some. All those fighting the fire did a wonderful job and I'd stand in awe as the water bombers would fly over with all their repeated trips to refill with water. With their fight going well, they told me the fire was about 66 percent contained, but still burning.

At one of the daily meeting that was held to keep us current on the fire, we were told it had burned about 92 square miles. And guess what part was not contained yet? That's right! The part between it and me! So far 88 homes had burned and 109 out buildings. But at last, with the rain and a lot of hard work, the fire was out and those of us who had been blessed with no damage gave prayers of thanks. Little did I know this would not be the last forest fire I'd have to deal with!

CHAPTER 21

Time For A Break!

Bears continued to be a problem even after the fire was out. With the fire having pushed several into my neck of the woods, a Brown Bear mauled a pastor as he was out walking. A couple of neighbors had been chased but nobody was injured and about a block away one neighbor had two brownies follow her and her dog all the way home. Finally, the moose showed back up in the yard and about 200 yards away salmon were running in the stream so the bears had a lot to keep them fed. I brought Ally with me at all times or locked her in the cabin when gone because a few dogs had become bear snacks.

I took Ally to the vet because she had developed some massive bulges on her back. The doctor determined they were deep tissue bruises from her encounter with the moose that had ripped down her half-inch cable dog run. Apparently Ally had been bounced off the trees while on her run because there was no evidence she was kicked.

In *the Woodcutter's Moon*, "August," I started needing a headlamp about midnight when it was overcast. The outhouse was built and the cabin close to being occupiable. There was no time to put up siding. It would be stored under the cabin until summer. I had basically worked seven days a week trying to get it ready to move into before winter with just the one short time off when I went fishing.

I was reminded, in my daily quite time, what it says in the Biggest Book in Ecclesiastes 3:1-8 where it states there is a season for everything. I realized my life revolved around the seasons, there was no time clock to punch. I lived by a timepiece woven tightly together advancing with perfect time, a clock with many hands. Some of these hands were the bull moose in rut, geese in flight, planting of gardens, netting salmon, migration of herds, chopping of wood, mushing season, and other things that had become timepieces that I now know, all had their appointed season and gave my life balanced reason. Yes, Ecclesiastes 3:1-8 was definitely true.

There needs to be a time of rest and for the biggest part I had kept a schedule for rest and eating, as well as a time for the *Great Mystery*, daily. That's keeping first things first!

One night a friend called, waking me, asking if I wanted to help her butcher a moose that had been hit by a car. Being in a deep sleep, I thought she meant she was on the road hunting for a moose to shoot during the night and wanted some help. Well, that sounded rather illegal and I asked her why she was road hunting at night? I finally realized she did not want to poach (illegal hunting, killing, or capturing of wild animals) a moose but that a cow had been hit and its leg had been broken so the troopers had to shoot it.

It is written in the Biggest Book in Proverbs 27:10,

"Do not forsake your friend and your father's friend, and do not go to your brother's house in the day of your calamity. Better is a neighbor who is near than a brother who is far away." This was a chance to heed this wisdom so off I went. I was rather impressed by my friend and her knowledge on how to butcher. We both brought home some moose meat, I had fun, and I slept very well that next night. Something I could never figure out was why you are not allowed to keep a moose you hit with your car even if your car was totaled because it is the state's moose. And if you have to shoot one in defence of life and property, you must give the meat up as well. There are lists one can get on and when called, you have to act immediately to retrieve the meat or they will go to the next person on the list. This is how my friend had gotten the moose I helped butcher. She was on a call list. But when a moose just dies on your property, it becomes your moose and you have to deal with it even if you don't want it. Now how does THAT make any sense?

I soon found this new "Dog House" kept very warm with the diesel drip pot running on #1, which is the lowest setting its carburetor had. With the walls one foot thick, it retained the heat.

Time For A Break!

Ice was forming on the lakes and we had a few snows, but no more than three inches at a time. Fall was beautiful as usual, but short. I was almost ready for snow since I'd put the Bronco's snow tires on it and the winter tires on the Subaru I had just purchased. All the scrap wood from my building project had been burned and the *used meals depository*, "Out House," had a door on it. The next big push would be to start cutting the trees I had dropped and stacked for firewood as I burned the brush piles. I also needed the ground cleared for next years garden and the archery range.

I had always wanted my own place to practice archery, especially since the *Great Mystery* had blessed me with my compound bow, a story that has the fingerprints of the *Great Mystery* all over it.

Time For A Break!

CHAPTER 22

It Was (Another) God Thing

Before coming to Alaska, I got in my truck one morning to make the hours drive to work. I was so broke it was a struggle buying groceries. I'd sold almost all my hunting gear and was really depressed about it since it had taken years to purchase my hunting rifles. I only had one rifle left. It was a left handed Savage bolt action in 243 Winchester with a fixed four power scope.

It Was (Another) God Thing

I had always wanted a compound bow, but as a lefty (left handed) and since only my left eye sees correctly, these types of bows are expensive and hard to find. That morning I said out loud, "You know, Great Father, I'd really like to have a compound bow to take with me to Alaska but there is no way I could ever afford one. I can't even find an archery shop that has a left handed one within miles of me." That was all I said.

About three weeks earlier, I had run into an old friend who I had not seen for several years. The night we had agreed for him to come over for coffee just happened to be the same day I had made my odd, little prayer on my way to work. When he came over, the first thing out of his mouth was "do you know anybody who would have a left handed Savage bolt action in 243 Winchester with a fixed four power scope. I've hurt my shoulder and can no longer pull the string on my left handed compound bow and I'd like to do a swap. I have a nice case for it along with the arrows and many other archery things I'll throw in to boot. My bow is really nice. I bought the best I could find." My mouth dropped. I told him my story and how I had just told the Father my desire that morning. I told him I had what he was looking for. We agreed that night to trade with each other. A few days later, with neither of us having seen the others equipment, we swapped out. We were both very pleased. Yes, it was a "God Thing."

I started looking for five dogs. I needed a good lead dog (often females, usually noted for their high level of intelligence and drive); two swing dogs (the two dogs directly behind the lead, and two wheel dogs (the two right in front of the sled and normally the strongest in the team).

I had enough left over wood to build the dog houses but then decided to build just one big dog house. I started clearing out trees for a dog yard, building an eight foot high fence. I wanted my team to be able to roam free and not be chained up.

Soon it was *the Moon of the Popping Trees*, "December," and my Mum was coming for Christmas, expecting a dog sled ride, and not having a team yet, I lined up a ride for her. One of the teams I took care of when their owners were on vacation said they would take her out. Little did I know that same team would eventually be singing in my own dog yard!

It Was (Another) God Thing

Soon it was the Christmas season with temperatures dropping down to 20 degrees below or colder at night. Mum flew in, making my holiday very enjoyable. We were going to visit Homer and Fairbanks, as well as tour my world. The trip to Fairbanks was a great time to talk about the real reason for the season, the birth of Yiissus, the Christ.

Mum had her dog sled ride, visited and ate true Alaskan chow with many of my friends, and shopped, doing the normal tourist things. Of course, although we looked, she did not see one single moose on the Kenai which normally has them all over the place. However, we did spot a couple of cows with their calves near Fairbanks way off in the distance. Fairbanks has great Northern Lights, unless you want your Mum to view them. The night we drove up to Fairbanks, it clouded up and stayed overcast until the night we drove out of town. Two nights after she flew home, right here in my back yard, the lights gave a great showing. And, the day after I took her to the airport, I counted 17 moose on the 3-1/2 mile stretch of road that connects my home from the highway. I just had to laugh.

CHAPTER 23

And So Went The Winter

That first winter I had a rather unique and unforgettable experience. Since I do not drink alcohol, I wear my hair long and do not cut it because it is a sign that I do not partake. Some First Nation's people follow this practice. It was cold so when I laid down in my sleeping bag, I decided to zip it all the way to the top rather than half way up like I normally did. All semed to go well until I tried moving my head, finding a pile of my hair had somehow become zipped into the zipper about six inches from the top of the zipper. With a little work I reached out the top and felt what appeared to be just about every single hair on my head in the zipper. The zipper did not want to zip down and my hair did not want to pull out. I had gone to bed about 11:00 P.M. and finally got out about midnight. I was in that mess for over an hour! I am blessed I am not claustrophobic (a fear of small, enclosed spaces) like my Mum.

Everything I could see was covered in a thick layer of hoarfrost. Sparkling like diamonds, my trees looked like something from an enchanted fairytale. As the cold temperatures settled in deeper, I could hear trees popping and the lake ice groaning.

A pack of wolves had been active so I could not leave Ally out on her run when I was not home. Even at 130 pounds and as fierce as she could be, there would be no chance for survival against a wolf pack and wolves do feast on dogs here in Alaska.

I soon began hearing a pair of owls calling on most nights. They lived in the spruce forest close to the cabin. The bears that had run around the neighborhood were finally starting to bed down for winter. My moose were back all the time now and a fox kept poking its head around the cabin, sometimes barking.

I was heating the cabin with my oil drip stove which put out 35,000 BTU when cranked up all the way. It was drinking about five gallons of stove oil a day (that's right, five gallons a DAY) when running on high in extreme cold, which put a big bite in the old pocket book. I decided an airtight woodstove, which puts out way more BTU, would be the way to heat the place and it would be a lot cheaper since trees that could be harvested were plentiful on the Kenai. I started looking for a good stove and Oslie, a buddy of mine from the Lower-49, found me one. We just needed to ship it up.

Because I relied on my oil stove for heat and had gotten some bad fuel that was freezing up, one night I had to go get a friend to help me unthaw my fuel line leading to the stove. On this trip over I found Bullwinkle in a heavy blizzard. I was just driving along and this flying moose decided to land on its back in the Subaru's front seats. The only problem it encountered was the windshield, top of the car, and a dashboard. The next thing I knew, the ambulance was there and my lovely Subaru, which was just crushed, was being hauled away and not to my homestead. I was told they expected to total the little station wagon I had just recently purchased. I was bummed! I was blessed with just having a few cuts and a whiplash, but this gave me my fourth concussion and it was a slow comeback.

The State Trooper was amazed I was not more critically injured. Bullwinkle got up and dragged himself into the woods, keeping out of effective range of the trooper's handgun that could have put him out of his misery. The trooper got tired of wading through the deep snow and gave him up for the wolves.

Even in this, I was able to see the fingerprints of the *Great Mystery*. Normally I wear contacts but before I left the cabin, I decided to wear my glasses instead. The impact of the moose hitting the windshield caused it to shatter into such tiny pieces that my glasses looked like they were covered in snow. If I had been wearing my contacts, I would have permanently lost my eyesight. Once again I was given the assurance that I was being cared for and watched over.

How true the verse is in 1 Thessalonians 5:18 that says, "…give thanks in all circumstances; for this is the will of God in Christ Jesus for you." It does not say give thanks "for" the circumstances but "in" the circumstances. My eyesight had been spared and for that I had much for which to be thankful and to offer deep, heartfelt praises and thanksgiving to my Father, the *Great Mystery*, Who once again had revealed just how much He loves me.

Oslie and two other friends, Gene and Kern, crated and shipped to me a woodstove. Before long it was sending smoke up the chimney. I only loaded it twice a day and even dampering it down so I wouldn't roast, I still had to sleep with windows open.

About that time the owner of the team that had given my Mum a ride called. "Would you be interested in my seven, middle-aged, Siberian sled dogs? If you are, you have to agree to take them by this coming winter." Without any hesitation I said, "yes!"

And So Went The Winter

CHAPTER 24

The Team

I n Alaska you look out the window before opening the door. After opening it, you look deeply into the woods before stepping outside. Many, who have not made this a practice, have been badly hurt or worse. I always watch for bears, moose, and wolves who rarely come down from the Caribou Hills, but sometimes I have encountered them within sight of the cabin.

The Team

My biggest concern, if having a severely hard winter, has always been the wolves I had encountered on the trails while mushing. In hard times they have come into homesteads, killing dogs for food and attacking people. I personally know more than one who has been attacked.

Since the roof of the cabin was very high and still covered with snow, making the metal roof very slick, I was not able to clean the smoke stack like I needed. Consequently, it built up creosote (a dark brown or black flammable tar deposited from wood smoke on the walls of a chimney) inside the smoke stack and one night I had the fire department out. My stovepipe went from the color black, to red, and then to white. I was very pleased I had built within the 5-mile radius the fire station serves. By the time they got there, I'd put the fire out but that was not going to happen again if I could help it. I installed a ring to attach a climbing rope so I could get into a harness (a combination of straps, bands, and other parts that form a 'safety' belt a person wears to keep them safe when in high places) and with someone on the other end of the rope, help keep me up on the roof to clean, as needed, the smoke stack.

The Team

Since most mushers I knew fed their dog teams heavily on meat and fish, I did as many of them do and started collecting from people their last seasons moose, caribou, salmon, and halibut. The majority of it was vacuum packed and much of it was in perfect enough condition for even my consumption. By *the Moon When the Ice Goes Out of the Rivers*, "May," I had collected three used freezers and had them stuffed full of meat and fish as people dumped on me their last years frozen in preparation for that years harvest. The dogs being given to me came with one freezer and between the old "Dog House " and the new cabin, which I also called the "Dog House," I had room for all four freezers. Since fish brings in bears, I normally feed meat only in winter, after the bears hibernate.

The seven dogs turned into six just before I brought them home because one died in his sleep. I was bummed but glad he did not suffer. I started spending a little more time with them, visiting them often. I had figured the neighbors would hate the sound of a dog team, but I was wrong. They were noisy only when they were being fed or hooked up to the sled. Otherwise, they were quite, an exception being when they sang to the moon or another dog team.

The Team

After I'd brought my team home, I'd go out on the porch some nights and in the far off distance I'd hear a team singing. Then, in order, three other teams would sing and finally my team would complete the session. I used to tell people that Huskies howl, but my Siberian Huskies sing.

Keedah, the queen of the pack and mother of all the dogs, was old. I was asked if they could keep her for a pet. I agreed. My five dogs, Tiko, Pedro, Denali, Haicho and Cody would haul me nicely.

I started going to dog shows and meeting other mushers, looking for more Siberians. I was very quickly told that I did not have girl or female dogs or boy or male dogs. That the "proper" name for the females was "bitch" and the proper name for the males was either "sires" or "bastards." It took me a little time to get used to this since two of the names, if used when I was a kid at home, would have brought me discipline from my Mum.

The team came with a beautiful taboggan style dog sled, not a basket style. There were tuglines, necklines, harnesses, headlamps, bungies, snow hooks, snublines, a cooking pot for

The Team

trail use, booties and extra of everything including a dog crossing sign, a freezer full of meat, and much more. They were coming with everything a new musher could desire and since they were all seasoned veterans, they would be able to train me.

Unlike many teams that lived on chains, this team all lived in one big dog house. At feeding time they would line up and as I set their bowls down, the dogs knew their order and would come up and eat when their bowl was set down. They did not fight over the other's food bowls. They were just fun loving, happy dogs that were a blessing to own, especially since I'd only ridden a sled once for that one race and I was still pretty clueless!

The Team

CHAPTER 25

Just Every Day Alaska Living

Soon the first green grass of spring appeared, then the new leaves. The first moose calves were soon playing in the yard and another bear was shot on my road after it charged a man.

When all the trees had been cleared for the dog yard and all posts were in place, I surrounded it with an eight foot fence.

My neighbor and fellow musher, Jill, had a big Brown Bear come right into her dog yard. It had to be shot with rubber shot gun slugs to make it leave. I placed an electric fence at different levels around the dog yard to keep bears out. It ran off a battery and only needed charged about every three months.

In *the Moon of Making Fat*, "June," a Hairy Woodpecker, "Picoides villosus," came to live on the property. It would wake me up almost every morning trying to put holes in the metal roof. As the day went on he would go to work on some of the beetle kill trees, but throughout the day he'd be back to rattle the roof. He reminded me of Acts 26:14 when the Apostle Paul was telling of his conversion to Yiissus. It says in the last part of that verse, "It is hard for you to kick against the goads." Now a goad was a long pointed stick that was used to poke cattle to get them to move where you wanted them to go. To kick a goad would cause pain. It is better to just do what one should do in following the right path instead of insisting on beating off ones "beak" against something that will not help you. This just brings headace to your life and does not produce positive results. To do what the *Great Mystery* desires will bring success, not doing so will bring pain as you kick against the goad.

One night, much to my surprise, I noticed some Little Brown Bats, "Myotis lucifigus," darting this way and that. I had not realized bats lived in Alaska. Since they eat way more than their weight in mosquitoes each night, I made sure I did not close up all the spaces where they could roost in the cabin because they were going to be a help.

One thing that helped with expenses is that I started doing my laundry at home. I bought a washboard and galvanized wash tube and heated water on the woodstove. Then I'd wring my clothes out and either hang them outside, weather permitting, or build a fire in the cabin, hanging them up to dry. In the winter I'd often hang them outside and let them freeze dry. When I'd take them off the clothes line, they would be as stiff as a board. I had to be careful because at times, when I was in a hurry, I have actually broken tee shirts that were frozen.

Because I try to eat a healthy diet, I started grinding all my own grains to make flour for my bread, waffles, pancakes, muffins, and cookies. I purchased a handcrank grain mill that worked great. It was wonderful filling the cabin with the smell of fresh baked goods.

I found that cast-iron bread pans or drop biscuit pans were just the ticket. And, a cast-iron Dutch oven was perfect for Spruce grouse, "Falcipennis canadensis," hare, muskrat, "Ondatra zibethicus," stews, and black bean chilli. Often I'd put a dish into the Dutch oven in the morning and place it on the woodstove. When I left for the day I'd load the stove, damper it down, and when I got home, dinner was waiting. It was just that easy.

One night three of my good friends came for dinner. As we ate, Ally just sat and stared at one of them with her full attention. This started to make my friend feel a little uncomfortable because Ally was one tough dog to just have sit and stare at you. He finally voiced his concern and I told him, "relax, nothing is going to happen. I just didn't have enough big bowls for everyone so I washed out her bowl and you are eating out of it." The look on his face was priceless. The upside was that after dinner I did not need to wash his bowl, Ally did the job very well for me.

Soon it was *the Red Salmon Time Moon*, "July," when a local musher, whose team I could hear in the distance, asked me to start working that summer for her as a dog handler. Since it was just a couple of miles drive from my cabin, I started feeding and cleaning up after the "Red Shed Racing" team. Jill, the musher, was later featured in People's Magazine. I found her dog yard rather unique. I do not remember how many dogs made up this team of rescued dogs she had collected from other mushers or from the local animal shelter. They had a very large dog yard where they all had a private dog house next to which they were chained, daily. But every night all these dogs were brought inside the cabin to sleep, and her cabin was not much bigger than the one I was now sleeping in. Can you imagine trying to sleep with all those dogs snoring? I only helped out that summer but it was an interesting way to see dogs kenneled.

That summer I went through the first earthquake since I'd built the cabin. It made the cabin dance. About that time a volcano blew its top and I felt my best shake yet. The ash cloud was noticeable so I headed to town where I tried to buy dust masks for myself and extra air filters for both vehicles. Neither masks nor filters were available because there had been a rush on existing supplies. I placed a call to my Mum for an overnight shipment of masks and filters to be expressed to me from the Lower-49. I was able to buy panty hose, which I placed over the vehicles air intakes, to work as a pre-filter. This was a normal thing to carry for just such a circumstance in this part of Alaska and to this day I keep them stowed away along with the road flares and jumper cables. All the ash made the moon rise just beautiful but brought to mind what it says in the Biggest Book in Revelations concerning the final days.

CHAPTER 26

If I Had Only Stopped To Listen

The closest lake to my cabin was Johnson Lake and it was full of trout! Although I did well fishing from the bank, I decided I wanted a boat to get me out a little further where I had observed the big ones jumping. For a few dollars, I bought a garage sale 11-foot crawdad boat by the Coleman Company. A small electric trolling motor that ran off a deep cycle marine battery powered this small plastic boat. I named it the H.M.S. (Her Majesties Service) Ally. It was just the ticket for trolling for fish near the lily pads toward the middle of the lake.

Ally took to riding in the bow (the front end) of the boat, stretching out as I plowed around the lake. Soon I was fishing several lakes for trout since I enjoyed fishing for trout more than salmon. I often pondered, while sitting on the lake, the story in the Biggest Book in Matthew 17:24-27 where the Messiah sent Peter out to catch a fish that would have a shekel in its mouth so Peter could pay their Temple Tax. I just wonder what Peter was thinking while fishing for that fish, and I'd like to have seen his face when he took the shekel out of its mouth. Did he then release the fish or keep it?

At the start of *the Moon of Leaves Turning Color*, "September," I placed the boat on top of my Bronco and Ally and I headed to Engineer Lake. We were going to cross the lake and camp at a cabin for the night. It was a beautiful fall afternoon when I loaded the boat with all the gear and food. Ally took up her spot on the bow of the boat and we were soon gliding across the lake that was as smooth as glass, the water reflecting the surrounding landscape. That evening we sat around the fire and eventually I crawled into my sleeping bag, Ally laying beside me with her head facing the door as she usually did. Any sound in the night brought her to full attention as she would listen intently, and every once in a while she would get up and peer out the windows. I had never really seen her show any fear. She was just a calm, four legged angel as far as I was concerned.

I woke to the cabin being pelted by rain as the wind started picking up. Looking out over the lake I could see it was starting to get a little choppy, a far cry from the tranquil mirror it had been the previous day. Since it was obviously getting worse, I decided it was time to leave as fast as we could before the lake became too rough to navigate. We should have stayed put!

Since I always wore a life preserver, I quickly put it on and within minutes the boat was running as fast as the little trolling motor could push us. We were doing well until we came around a bend in the lake and were hit with such hard winds and waves I was concerned we would start taking on water. I had to keep the bow into the wind because this storm was now way beyond unsafe. I realized it had been a mistake to try to leave the safety of the cabin. I needed Divine help to keep the small boat from capsizing. Ally panicked, the only time I had ever seen her do such a thing, and she came back to me, leaning against me for all she was worth. This was a plus because without her added weight in the bow, the boat sat higher in the rough water as we crashed into the waves. We would run wide open into the waves and then at just the right moment turn and run in the needed direction to get us back to the landing for just a few moments and then quickly turn back into the waves before we took on more water. There was no real good place to beach the boat or I would have. I noticed the trolling motor was starting to slow. The fierce waters were giving it a workout I had not anticipated.

I was praying to the *Great Mystery*, asking that Ally and I be spared just like the story where the Son of God calmed the storm in Luke 8:22-25. I believe I really understood how the disciples felt when they yelled, "Master, Master, we are perishing!" For although I had on my life vest, I realized that as cold as this water was, if this boat went down, I'd likely die from hypothermia (when your body temperature gets so

dangerously low you could seriously hurt yourself or die). Totally soaked, after what seemed like an eternity, we made it back to the boat launch and when we were within swimming distance, Ally bailed out and swam to shore.

The trolling motor was almost dead. Later, at home, I found the battery was so far gone it would not have been able to propel us for another five minutes. The *Great Mystery* had His fingerprints all over this. Although He had not stilled the storm, He gave the trolling motor enough power and me the quick reflexes to help fight the waves and make it back to land. Yes, He saved Ally and me that day just like He saved His disciples the day He calmed their storm.

The thought occured to me that this was a life lesson as well. How many times had I been safe where I was but decided I wanted to rush into the storm of life to acomplish something? If I had sought the whisper of the *Great Mystery* that morning, might He have told me to just sit and wait out the storm rather than take a chance? I would not have been trying to bail water out of the boat with a bucket in one hand while steering it with the other. And, although He protected Ally and me in spite of my foolishness, was I unwittingly trying to test Him because I was doing what I wanted that day? It is written in the Biggest Book in Deuteronomy 6:16: "You shall not put the Lord your God to the test."

If I Had Only Stopped To Listen

CHAPTER 27

And Then... Finally!!

At the end of *the Moon of Leaves Turning Color,* "September," I went to pick up my dog team. It was one of the most exciting days of my life. I borrowed a dog truck and soon the dogs were in their new dog yard and my "new to me" dog sled was sitting in my living room. It made a great footstool. The dogs were getting used to their new dog yard and were quiet most of the day. But each

And Then... Finally!!

morning between 6:00 and 7:00 they would start to sing to the other dog teams in the distance. I loved their song, but would my neighbors? As it turned out, they did.

One night, when I opened the gate to feed the team, Haicho, my dominant sire, decided to make a run at Ally who was on her cable run. He leaped high to clear the electric fence just inside the gate, bolting toward her like lighting. When the two collided, Haicho was hit so hard you would have thought a sledge hammer hit his chest. As he flipped backwards onto his back from the force of his charge, Ally was right on top of him. He did not stand a chance because at 60 pounds, Ally outweighed him by 70 pounds. Fortunately for him, Ally listens very well to me or she probably would have put a massive hurt on him. After I called her off, he bolted for the safety of the dog yard. Never again did he or any other dog make such an unwise move.

I would soon start running them in front of a four-wheeler. It is wonderful to watch your dreams unfold. I asked the *Great Mystery* for more snow that coming winter than any normal person would ever dream of having.

And Then... Finally!!

Being blessed with good connections, my team ate for almost free. People gave me pounds of moose, caribou, fish, and other meats, all from the previous years hunting and fishing. Soon my freezers were full so I passed the extra on to other mushers. Once you get on a list with people, it becomes a yearly thing.

Because there are so many sled dogs in Alaska, every year many areas set a day to give their necessary shots at a reasonable price. They do not want health problems developing that would hurt mushing, the recognized state sport of Alaska. Just show up at an appointed day with your team and they get vaccinated.

My biggest cost would be trucking them to trailheads. Most of the time I just mushed them out of the yard. A friend bought a new dog truck and then gave me his old one. It was a rust bucket averaging about six miles per gallon of gas. It was beyond ugly. One door had to be held shut with a large bungee cord and I could see the road through the rusted out floorboard. But to me, it was a treasure sent by the hand of the *Great Mystery* so when I had extra gas money, I could transport my

And Then... Finally!!

team to different trailheads to mush. But most importantly, if another forest fire required evacuation, I could load my dogs and simply drive away to safety. My dogs were more than animals, they were my family, a gift from the *Great Mystery*. With this four-wheel drive, 24-dog team truck, I could also take all my gear, putting the sled on top. And, if I had to flee, there would be room for tools and personal stuff.

Soon the rainy, fall season descended and I was able to start running my new family. The rain helped the team stay cool and not over heat. It is hard on a dog to run when too warm because of their fur coat. If they over heat, it can affect them for life, much like a person who has had heat stroke. Damage is never really undone and over time usually gets worse, eventually bringing death.

An hour and a half before a run, I would give them baited water (water with a little soaked kibble or meat juice in it so they would be sure to drink their fill of water). Although I feed mornings and evenings, dogs should not be fed a heavy meal before mushing because they, like people, do not run well after a big meal.

And Then… Finally!!

After their drinking, I stretched out the gangline to the front of the four-wheeler and attached it to a bungee and a safety line that I attached to the front of the four-wheeler. The safety line is always longer than the bungee because you want the dogs pulling against the bungee and not the safety line. That line is there in case the bungee fails so the dogs cannot run off without their musher.

I was extremely proud of Tiko, my lead dog, because he kept the team all lined out while I hooked up the harnesses. The gangline ran from the bungee to the back of the lead dogs harness. To line out meant I gave a command to the lead dog to keep this line taunt so I could attach the rest of the team. Then the other dogs were placed one at a time in the positions they ran, after they were harnessed, by first attaching the tuglines to the back of their harness and then the necklines to their collars. Since the tugline and the neckline were attached to the gangline, the dogs were not able to wander about. Because I had at first started mushing with a single leader, no neckline for the leader was needed, but when I added one more leader later that winter, a neckline was run between their collars.

And Then... Finally!!

With all of this attached in front of the four-wheeler, I was ready to yell the word, "hike!" Would they listen to me? They had never been with me anywhere before and I could only hope they would listen as they trained me to become their musher. As I had started hooking them up, the dogs began going berserk! They barked, screamed, and danced in place as they lunged forward. Some were bounding up into the air much like a Snowshoe hare. All the while, with four of the dogs acting like this was Christmas Eve, Tiko, my leader stood still, keeping the team stretched out.

After a short prayer in my driveway I barked out the command, "hike!" The five immediately became silent as they flew into action. As we tore off down the road I called out, "easy," and they slowed their stride for me. Did I remember all the commands I had decided to use? The only two commands that are universal in the world of mushing are "gee" and "haw." Gee means to go right, haw means go left. Would Tiko listen to me as I approached that first turn? Suddenly, as we approached, I observed him turn and look back over his shoulder to see what I wanted. I gave him the command, "haw," and turning his head in the forward position he guided the team

And Then… Finally!!

around the path I had chosen to run. Within half a mile I gave the same command once again as he looked over his shoulder to me, and just as before he executed the command with precession. Suddenly, there was an intersection I had not thought about. I decided I wanted to take the team to the right. Would he do this? As he looked back, I barked the command, "gee," and just as flawlessly he turned the team in that direction.

As we ran down the long, straight stretch, it dawned on me that I needed to do more than just give the commands I wanted my dogs to follow. The *Great Mystery* did more than that to me. Out of His love for me He, in many ways, brought countless words of encouragement and praise. It says in the Biggest Book in Zephaniah 3:17 that the *Great Mystery*, the Indescribable Three in One, even sings over us. So then and there I made the decision I would follow suit. After every given command that Tiko did correctly, I gave him praise. As an example, if I called out "gee" and he did as directed, when in the middle of the swing to the right and after completely through that turn, I called out "good gee, Tiko, good gee, boy." I was able to watch his body language and started noticing it seemed to change, almost as if he had more pride.

And Then… Finally!!

Many say pride is a bad thing, that pride comes before a fall. And it is true that false pride or pride misdirected is not a healthy thing. But this word has another side, a good side. Webster's New World Dictionary says this about the word pride: "A proper respect for oneself; sense of one's own dignity or worth; self respect. Delight or satisfaction in one's own or another's achievements, in associations." As an example, I am proud I am a child of the *Great Mystery*, I am proud that I am part North American Indian. I now have a proper healthy sense of my own worth so it is easier to show myself respect. This is the type of pride I saw come alive in the dogs. As we ran, I would often praise each dog by name, and I sang Native songs to them as we glided along the paths, often under the Northern Lights. And with all of this, plus a lot of pats, rubs, and scratches, the team bonded to me like super glue, trying always to please me.

Since mushers use different kinds of commands, I decided to stick with the commands this team was familiar with. I used "all-right" to get them ready to mush and "hike" to get us to launch out on the trails. When I wanted them to pass something like a moose, or a driveway, I'd say "on-by" and the dogs would pass. When approaching an on-coming team,

And Then… Finally!!

I'd call out "gee-on-by" which meant I wanted them to stay to the right side of the trail and just pass by the other team. To speed them up, I'd call out "hike, hike" and they would pick up speed. To slow them I'd say "easy." And if I wanted them to stop I'd call out "whoa." When stopping along the trail, I'd call out "lineout" to have them keep their gangline stretched out. The hardest command for them to learn to follow was "whoa." They loved to run and rarely wanted to stop. This is a common problem for mushers.

They liked to sing and I always let them, at times howling along with them. But, when they barked at moose, other dogs, and who knows what else, I wouldn't put up with it. Their previous owner told me they hated the sound of a bee-bee gun. When fired against their barn, the noise frightened them. They were not being shot at but a whop sound could be heard when the bee-bee's hit the wooden barn. Just the sound of the bee-bees rolling around inside the gun when it was shaken was enough to silence them. I did not want to buy a bee-bee gun so I found a similar sound. Taking my Native American rain stick and flipping it, the sound was a lot like bee-bees shifting in a bee-bee gun. All the dogs would quit barking right away.

And Then… Finally!!

I started running them with the four-wheeler two days on and then one day off. Before every run I would eat a grilled cheese sandwich cut in chunks with maple syrup all over it. It became pretty much the meal I almost always ate before mushing.

I soon added a new dog, my first Alaskan Husky, named Prozac. The closest thing I can compare him to is Tigger in Winnie the Poo, except he was much worse. A few years later I'd end up with his brother who was just as amped up. Both, it turned out, would become excellent leaders.

By the end of *the Moon of Falling Leaves*, "October," I woke to a world covered in white. I was in Heaven. It had been snowing off and on since the first week of this *Moon of Falling Leaves* but the snow had not been sticking. I so hoped the snow would stick in the low country because the cost of gas getting the dogs up to the higher Caribou Hills was horrific. With the truck getting only six miles to the gallon, I was not going to be driving them very far, very often!

As the days became shorter and it slipped into a world of cold, snow, and ice, I heard the sound of the lake as it started to

And Then… Finally!!

freeze hard. The moaning that floated upon the breeze brought on by the lakes freeze-up brought this musher much anticipated excitement. Well, I called myself a musher but… was I? I had ridden a sled only once in a race that I had not planned to be in. Now here I was, still mushing my dogs with the four-wheeler as I waited for the snow to build up. I had all the equipment, and most of all I was the proud owner of a small team of six dogs that I had bonded with. I decided I was a musher.

I'd sit in the warmth of my cabin watching the fire burn while drinking steaming mugs of either tea or coffee with the window slightly open as I listened to the music of the creation. Yes, life was good and a gift from the *Great Mystery*. At night I could not decide if the lake moaning or the owl calling was my favorite sound.

I kept busy during the days that were growing shorter. I played with my dogs, mushing them by four-wheeler, split and stacked firewood, cleaned the dog yard twice daily, and put new hinges and latches on the dog truck along with other maintance it needed as I watched, with much anticipation, the snow build on the ground.

And Then... Finally!!

Finally the day came when I received news the first dog teams were on the trail I wanted to run. I decided I would mush that night and even though I did not have a mushing buddy and a mentor yet, I was determined to just go for it. I was told this trail was full of never ending hills so I decided I'd mush at night in order to see the oncoming lights from the snowmobiles when they were on the other side of a hill. That way I could stop the team and avoid a possible head-on which could be disastrous. During the day, I reasoned, I'd have no way of knowing I was on a possible collision course because with my fur beaver hat on, I'd not be able to hear the snowmobiles as they approached.

I readied all for the two and a half mile trip to the trailhead. I gathered up all needed equipment plus some extras including snacks for the dogs but that night they got salmon treats. I loaded a first aid kit, headlamp with extra batteries, a musher's knife that had a marlinspike to help loosen knots and was serrated for the quick cutting of lines in case of emergencies. I had extra mittens and liner gloves, snacks for me and a thermos of hot tea, snowshoes, an ax, matches, fire starter, and a road flare to start a fire in an emergency. And just in

And Then… Finally!!

case, I placed in the nose of the sled a very warm sleeping bag and the 12-gauge filled out the list.

I drove to the trailhead after loading the dogs. I had never seen them so excited. I found a good place to park where I could use the truck as the fixture I could attach the quick release to. (Since a dog team can possibly jerk loose the snow hooks, when possible a musher uses a quick release for added security. It is a line that runs from where the trace or gang line attaches to the front of a sled back to where the musher can reach it while standing on the sleds runners. The musher attaches the other end to a fixed object such as a dog truck, a tree or post. It works like an anchor. When the musher pulls the snow hooks, he then pulls the quick release from whatever he had it anchored to, allowing the dog team to move forward). I said a prayer and then, unloading the sled from the top of the dog truck, I attached all the needed lines to it. Both snow hooks were stomped into the snow and the quick release to the back bumper.

Tiko was harnessed first and placed in first position, and then Prozac joined him in lead. I gave the command "lineout"

And Then... Finally!!

and they did. The other dogs were soon placed in their normal positions. All the while, my lead dogs kept every one lined out.

I slipped on my mittens, looked toward the night sky that was close to a full moon and smiled before the *Great Mystery*. He had granted me this dream and I was confident He would mush with me along this trail. It was so bright with the moonlight upon the snow I did not need a headlamp, but I put it on just so I could signal a snowmobiler, if necessary, that I was on the trail. But until needed, I kept it turned off. Going to the front of the team, one by one I gave each of them words of encouragement as I rubbed their beautiful coats that shined beneath the moon.

Going to the sled I stood upon the runners as I lowered my drag mat. (A drag mat is used for helping to slow or steer the sled). I also tested the brake and it sliced deep into the snow. Then, keeping the brake set, I pulled the first snow hook. The dogs were all going berserk and were screaming with anticipation as they were all lunging forward. Was I ready for this since this was my first real run with no support whatsoever? I pulled the second snow hook and placed it in its proper

And Then… Finally!!

stowed position. Reaching for the quick release I gripped the handle bar with my other mitten so hard it almost hurt. Then, with my eyes peering over my six best friends on earth and the trail before me that was to quickly make a turn and plummet downward, I barked "hike!" as I yanked the quick release and before I could fill my lungs with one more breath, the sled launched with a ferocity that stunned me as we rocketed into the Alaskan Bush!